Praise for *Quie*...

'This is a quietly powerful book ... t[...] [...] Megumi's quietly powerful talk. It is comfortable, present and purposeful – providing authentic and thoughtful observations and collaborating with the reader to empower and celebrate their quietly powerful selves.'
Dr Steve Hodgkinson, CIO, Business Technology and Information Management, Corporate Services at Department of Health and Human Services

'Megumi Miki has written a must-read guide that flips our thinking about how powerful quietness can be in organisations. Packed with valuable advice drawn for personal experiences and interviews, this book is essential reading for those who tend to be quieter (and they are not only introverts) or those who want to leverage talent to get the most from quieter employees.'
Siobhan McHale, EGM People, Culture & Change at DuluxGroup and author of *The Insider's Guide to Culture Change*

'We live in a world that glorifies overconfidence and celebrates those who are unaware of their limitations. But there's a better way, as this timely book shows: stop overlooking humble, quiet, altruistic people for leadership roles, and we will all win.'
Dr Tomas Chamorro-Premuzic, psychologist, entrepreneur, TED speaker and author of 10 books including *Why Do So Many Incompetent Men Become Leaders?* and *The Talent Delusion*

'Megumi challenges our thinking to see how our quietness can be a leadership strength. She has put words to what I was subconsciously doing over many years in leadership positions. She shares important messages for organisations wishing to lift the quality of their leadership and embrace diversity in leadership styles by expanding their beliefs about good leadership. A quietly powerful approach to leadership allows everyone to shine, not just the leader.'

Ruth Picker, Partner at Ernst & Young, Asia Pacific Risk Management Lead and Songwriter

'Megumi brilliantly captures some very important and challenging ideas in organisational life with a central premise that people can be quiet while contributing powerfully and significantly. Through her indepth exploration, case studies and personal sharing, Megumi brings forward the contributions quietly powerfully people make and how, through our cultural bias, we do not give credit to those who are due this recognition. This book challenges how easily we overlook these important "leaders" and encourages us to re-examine who we value in organisations. This book is an important read for all leaders who'd like to optimise their hidden talent.'

Stephen Schuitevoerder, PhD, International consultant and facilitator in individual and systemic change, Board Chair of the Process Work Institute

'I truly believe the future needs all of us – loud, quiet, young, old. It also requires the best of us. Megumi has added something special to the inclusiveness and diversity agenda with *Quietly Powerful*.'

Matt Church, professional speaker, voted Top 10 Conference Speakers Globally, Founder and Chairman of Thought Leader Business School

'Having worked with a quietly powerful leader whom I admire greatly, I support Megumi's view that we need more of this kind of leader. As an introverted leader, I love the practical strategies which Megumi offers for quiet professionals to tap into their leadership strengths without feeling like they have to pretend to be someone they're not.'

Michelle Cornish, Senior Executive Coach, Learning Group Facilitator, Former Senior Executive Service Band 2 leader with a number of Commonwealth Government Departments

'Megumi is the consummate quietly powerful leader. Her book beautifully encapsulates her thought leadership in the topic. Peppered with her own insights and case studies, this book reassures and reaffirms how quiet leaders can use their unique qualities to lead with compassion and strength. In a world full of chaos, noise and complexity, this is a timely book reminding us not to overlook the power and possibility of quiet.'

Dr Jenny Brockis, Lifestyle Physician, professional speaker and author specialising in nurturing thriving teams and leaders

'As a quiet Asian leader, there is so much in Megumi's writing and insights that speaks to me gently, reassuringly and powerfully. She's been there before, herself, and lived a shared journey as a quietly powerful leader in a world that exalts extroversion and the extravagant. Megumi's strategies and guidance have now given power to new voices that are in dialogue with my own inner critics!'

Richard Foy, Chief Archivist, Archives New Zealand

'*Quietly Powerful* explores the complexities of how people can become quiet and hidden, beyond introversion. It highlights the value of quietness, solitude and quieter approaches to leadership and shares the benefits of and practical strategies for quiet professionals to thrive in their careers while remaining authentic. A must-read for all to either develop their own quietly powerful leadership or that of their quiet team members.'

Katrina Webb, OAM, Paralympic Gold Medallist, international speaker, Leadership and Personal Mastery Consultant

'In a world where those who speak the loudest are heard over those who might have something more constructive to say, Megumi and her book are a breath of fresh air. Having led projects for over 25 years, I've come across many people who dominate some poorly run project meetings, almost just for the sake of it. Unfortunately, this can come at a cost. That cost is not hearing from those quieter people; those who think and reflect before speaking. This book can help those people whose voices deserve to be heard, yet are not quite sure how to go about it.'

Mark Lowy, Past President, Project Management Institute Melbourne Chapter; Principal, Guava Project Consulting, sessional university lecturer, board advisor

'A fascinating, insightful and practical book on the potential and power of quiet professionals. *Quietly Powerful* reframes the conventional view of "quiet" and challenges outdated perceptions of effective leadership. An essential read for anyone who has ever felt unseen, discounted, or bypassed due to their quieter nature, and for those not-so-quiet among us who are interested in discovering a better way of working and succeeding in our complex world.'

Diana Renner, co-founder of the Uncharted Leadership Institute, award-winning co-author of *Not Knowing: the art of turning uncertainty* and *Not Doing: the art of effortless action*.

'As an introverted CEO, I am definitely in the minority. I have been fortunate in my career to have mentors and champions who have recognised my potential, despite it being what Megumi would call quiet and hidden. I would have loved to have had this book 25 years ago, when I was first navigating the corporate world. For any introverts, this is critical reading on how to move from disempowered to quietly powerful without losing yourself. However, this book goes beyond introversion, and is equally applicable to extroverts who feel hidden. And, finally, anyone in a leadership position needs this book to understand the quieter half of their workforce and to take advantage of this diversity of thinking.'

Peter Cook, CEO, Thought Leaders

Megumi Miki

Quietly Powerful

How your quiet nature is your hidden leadership strength

First published in 2020 by Major Street Publishing Pty Ltd
PO Box 106, Highett, Vic. 3190
E: info@majorstreet.com.au W: majorstreet.com.au M: +61 421 707 983

© Megumi Miki 2020

Quantity sales. Special discounts are available on quantity purchases by corporations, associations and others. For details, contact Lesley Williams using the contact details above.

Individual sales. Major Street publications are available through most bookstores. They can also be ordered directly from Major Street's online bookstore at www.majorstreet.com.au.

Orders for university textbook/course adoption use. For orders of this nature, please contact Lesley Williams using the contact details above.

The moral rights of the author have been asserted.

A catalogue record for this book is available from the National Library of Australia.

ISBN: 978-0-6485159-5-1

All rights reserved. Except as permitted under *The Australian Copyright Act 1968* (for example, a fair dealing for the purposes of study, research, criticism or review), no part of this book may be reproduced, stored in a retrieval system, communicated or transmitted in any form or by any means without prior written permission. All inquiries should be made to the publisher.

Cover design by Simone Geary
Internal design by Production Works
Printed in Australia by Ovato, an Accredited ISO AS/NZS 14001:2004 Environmental Management System Printer.

10 9 8 7 6 5 4 3 2 1

Disclaimer: The material in this publication is in the nature of general comment only, and neither purports nor intends to be advice. Readers should not act on the basis of any matter in this publication without considering (and if appropriate taking) professional advice with due regard to their own particular circumstances. The author and publisher expressly disclaim all and any liability to any person, whether a purchaser of this publication or not, in respect of anything and the consequences of anything done or omitted to be done by any such person in reliance, whether whole or partial, upon the whole or any part of the contents of this publication.

Contents

Acknowledgements **ix**

Introduction **1**

Part I: The quiet wasteland 11
Chapter 1   The hidden waste **13**
Chapter 2   Leadership gap **22**
Chapter 3   Personal damage **43**

Part II: Talent in hiding 57
Chapter 4   Personality **59**
Chapter 5   Upbringing **69**
Chapter 6   Power dynamics: Minority and rank **80**
Chapter 7   Holding yourself back **92**

Part III: Disregard for quiet talent 99
Chapter 8   Biased and fooled **101**
Chapter 9   Outdated beliefs about leadership **113**
Chapter 10   Biased systems and processes **117**
Chapter 11   Time for an update **123**

Part IV: Quietly powerful leadership 131
Chapter 12   Quiet does not equal Quietly Powerful **133**
Chapter 13   Three key attributes **138**
Chapter 14   Quiet superpowers **153**
Chapter 15   The path to Quietly Powerful **158**
Chapter 16   Appreciate fully **171**
Chapter 17   Adapt purposefully **187**

Part V: For the not-so-quiet people and organisations 211
Chapter 18 'So what?' for organisations **213**
Chapter 19 'So what?' for not-so-quiet individuals **223**

My wish, in conclusion **227**

About the author **228**

Sources and further reading **229**

Index **239**

Acknowledgements

The *Quietly Powerful* leader interviewees have been an invaluable source of inspiration and insights for this book. I'd like to acknowledge them for generously sharing their time and experiences with me.

These 29 leaders are either people I have known and experienced as Quietly Powerful myself, or people who have been recommended to me by others who saw them as Quietly Powerful. Their stories, as well as how they showed up in the interviews, allowed me to draw out what attributes enable them to be powerful and successful leaders. They were unassuming and humble, and our conversations were sprinkled with self-deprecating humour. I believe their quieter attributes have been the key to their success and impact in their respective fields.

Thank you:

- Aneetha de Silva, Managing Director, Government at Aurecon
- Angie Paskevicius, CEO and Executive Director of Holyoake, Non-Executive Director on multiple boards, executive coach and speaker
- Anne Flanagan, former CFO at RACV, Director, AustralianSuper
- Brad Chan, CEO of Banna Property Group; Founder of Haymarket HQ
- Caroline Stainkamph, most recently Head of Business Management and Transformation at Computershare; Program Director at Vic ICT for Women

- Clive Peter, Manager, People & Culture at the City of Melbourne; formerly held a range of HR positions at ANZ, Ford, Shell and BHP
- Dianne Jacobs, Founding Principal – The Talent Advisors; former Partner, Goldman Sachs JBWere
- Elizabeth Proust, Chairman of Bank of Melbourne, Nestle Australia, former Chairman of the Australian Institute of Company Directors, 2010 Officer of the Order of Australia
- Fiona Adler, entrepreneur and third Australian woman to summit Everest
- Giovanni Stagno, most recently Partner at Ernst & Young, Asia Pacific Technology Risk Leader
- Helen Macfarlane, Partner, Addisons
- Jane Bird, Global IT Business Operations Manager at JR Simplot Australia
- Dr Jason Fox, Archwizard of The Cleverness, 2016 'Keynote Speaker of the Year', Pioneering Leadership & Motivation Design
- Dr Jenny Brockis, Medical Doctor, Speaker, author and Director of Brain Fit, specialising in brain health and high-performance thinking
- Katrina Webb, OAM, Paralympic gold medallist, international speaker, Leadership and Personal Mastery Consultant
- Kevin Larkins, Interim CEO of The Bodhi Bus, experienced senior executive and coach
- Lisa Evans, Director, Speaking Savvy, professional speaker, public Speaking and storytelling coach
- Liz Compton, Director People & Culture at Auto & General

Acknowledgements

- Mark Lowy, Past President, Project Management Institute Melbourne Chapter; Principal, Guava Project Consulting, Sessional University Lecturer, board advisor
- Michelle Grocock, Ironman and Executive General Manager, Internal Audit at National Australia Bank
- Oscar Trimboli, author of *Deep Listening* and *Breakthrough*, speaker and mentor
- Paul Boasman, Executive, Financial Strategy & Performance at Telstra
- Ruth Picker, Partner at Ernst & Young, Asia Pacific Risk Management Lead and Songwriter
- Simon Harrington, retired Rear Admiral with the Royal Australian Navy, Executive Coach and Mentor
- Stacey Barr, Performance Measure and KPI Specialist, author of *Prove It!* and *Practical Performance Measurement*, Creator of PuMP
- Dr Steve Hodgkinson, CIO, Victorian Department of Health and Human Services
- Susan Allen, formerly Executive General Manager at RACV, now Board Director
- Susan Middleditch, Deputy Secretary, Corporate & Regulatory Services at Victoria Police
- Yamini Naidu, Business Storyteller, speaker and author, the world's only economist turned storyteller.

I would also like to thank Lesley Williams of Major Street Publishing, who came to my Quietly Powerful talk and worked closely with me on everything from the book title to getting the entire book into shape.

A big thanks to my long-time friend, Diana Renner, who co-authored the thought-provoking books *Not Knowing* and *Not Doing*. She used her incredible mind to improve the flow and logic of this book. Her advice was invaluable, given her experience in writing, storytelling and knowledge in the field of leadership.

There are also countless numbers of people who have encouraged and supported me throughout the last few years as I experimented with the idea of *Quietly Powerful*. Some are close friends and colleagues; others are distant LinkedIn connections who sent unprompted messages to me. Every one of these supporters has kept me going with the work, especially as I struggled with the anxiety of being in the limelight. The irony of going public with the idea of being a quiet professional who doesn't like attention has not escaped me.

Two significant teachers who helped me to grow more into my authentic self have been Stephen Schuitevoerder and Gita Bellin. Thank you for seeing my potential and patiently helping me to grow. I'd also like to acknowledge the many teachers and thought leaders whose work has made me think and provided a solid base to build on. I've learned a great deal from the authors and speakers I refer to throughout the book, and their work continues to stretch my thinking.

Thank you to my husband, Aaron, who has read and given feedback on pretty much all my blog articles and the draft of this book. I am grateful to my family, who have been patient with me at times when I have been overly quiet and independent. Their trust and confidence in me give me the freedom to do what I love: to explore and expand myself.

Finally, thank you to my daughter, Sophia, for inspiring me to learn about one of the most quietly powerful art forms – classical ballet. Her passion rubbed off on me and I started adult ballet classes in 2016, allowing me to appreciate how strong, flexible and athletic you need to be to be a ballet dancer. Great dancers express so much with no words, and to me, that's incredibly powerful.

Introduction

The quiet girl who didn't fit in

I was only five years old when my family moved to Sydney from Japan. It was April and I had just finished kindergarten. While I was born in Melbourne during my father's first transfer to Australia, we'd returned to Japan when I was 18 months old, and the only English words I knew were 'yes', 'no' and 'toilet'.

I entered the wire gates of Turramurra Public School, holding my mother's hand, walking slightly behind her. It felt like a very big school with a very big playground, especially compared to kindergarten in Japan. We walked into a classroom and were greeted by the teacher. Lots of blue, green and brown eyes looked on as the teacher said something I didn't understand and pointed to two girls who were smiling at me. I didn't know what to say, but my mother left and the two girls came over and took my hand.

I didn't need to understand English to know what the kids meant when they made facial expressions and said, 'Eeew, what's that?' while pointing to the rice balls in my lunchbox. That afternoon I told my mother that I didn't want Japanese rice balls for lunch anymore. It was long before the days of sushi shops in every suburb. My daughter has had rice balls in her lunchbox since she started school eight years ago and she receives looks of envy from her friends!

A few weeks later, a boy came running over to me to pull the ends of his eyes up and down and yell out 'Chinese, Japanese!' I was the only Asian girl in my year level, so it was difficult to hide. It was the first time in my life that I realised I was not the same as everyone else – that I didn't fit in. While I didn't have a terrible time at that school, it was something of a relief to move to the Sydney Japanese International School two years later. In hindsight, years 3 and 4 at the Sydney Japanese International School were the only school years that I can say I really enjoyed.

We moved back to Kobe, Japan, when I started year 5. Surprisingly, it was just as difficult, if not more so, in Japan, particularly when I reached high school.

In year 5, I'd joined a swimming club in Kobe to train competitively, and at my peak I was swimming ten times a week. With that much training in a highly chlorinated pool, my hair started turning a reddish brown, and became lighter and lighter over time. My hair is naturally wavy, too, and the damage from the chlorine made it frizzy. In a school full of Japanese kids with black hair, I really stood out! High school rules were strict, and colouring, bleaching and perming your hair was not permitted. (There were also rules on the length of your uniform skirt and your hairstyle: it was the collectivist Japanese culture at its worst.) The 'naughty' kids used to deliberately bleach their hair to rebel against the school rules. So, you can imagine what the teachers thought of me!

Sure enough, I got pulled aside by the homeroom teacher in year 7. He told me off for bleaching my hair and, when I tried to explain that it was from swimming, he got angry. That night, my mother wrote a note to the teacher to explain the situation, and he stopped hassling me, but I felt like he was watching me all the time. I really had to blend in to avoid getting into trouble.

There was also the time when the popular girls in the class backed me into a corner in the schoolyard. They told me that I was a show-off for standing out with my hair, for speaking fluent Australian English in the English classes and for getting good marks in all the core subjects. After that, I started telling white lies about my marks, saying that they were around average, and playing dumb in the English classes, trying to speak with a Japanese-American accent. I stopped swimming altogether by the time I was 14. It was safer for me to be quiet and hidden.

Over the course of my childhood, my family continued moving around a lot, and in total I went to eight different schools in three countries. I became a master at blending in. Being quiet was a survival mechanism; it was also my natural tendency.

I am an introvert and have always been the quiet one. In Japanese, I was always told that I was *otonashii* – 'mild and meek'. If you look at the Japanese characters, however, they actually say 'adult-like', with connections to being honest, warm and rounded. I was praised for being calm, doing things at my own pace and handling pressure well – so being *otonashii* didn't feel like a bad thing.

Staying quiet and hidden was safe and felt natural. Standing out made life difficult.

Putting quietness to the side

After university in Adelaide, Australia, getting a job at a global management consulting firm was a shock to the system. As a twenty-something consultant, I was thrown in front of clients and expected to have intelligent conversations about their business. I had to look like I knew what I was doing, and I constantly worried about not knowing enough and being found out. I was expected to speak up in the presence of outspoken, articulate senior leaders – mostly white men – and to be considered for promotion to manager level, we had to make a presentation to a group of senior leaders and peers who knew more about the topic than we did. On top of that, we socialised regularly with our peer group, with an unwritten rule about working hard and playing hard.

To get through this, I had to find a way to look more polished and confident, fast. So, I worked long hours to be as well prepared as possible. I did professional development in areas such as presentation skills and relationship management. I learned to project my voice, to watch my 'ums' and 'ahs', how I stood, how I used my hands and where I looked. And I put on my suit and high heels, hoping I looked the part.

I stayed six years, learned a lot and completed some excellent and not-so-great projects, and burned out at the age of 29. I lasted six years, only because I was still in my twenties!

A few years later, I was fortunate enough to have the opportunity to make a big change in careers, with a job as a facilitator and consultant for an organisation-wide cultural transformation program at ANZ Bank, doing leadership and culture work. It was a dream job in terms of what it allowed me to learn, my passion for the topics and the feeling of making a positive difference.

However, it required me to stand in front of groups to present and facilitate most of the time. I had a difficult time taking off my 'professional' mask due to all the presentation techniques I'd learned, and regularly got told to 'be myself' and bring more energy. Other times I'd be told to 'be more confident' and develop my 'executive presence'. The feedback made more anxious and self-conscious, which made it even more difficult to be myself.

Being on the road and in front of groups so much exhausted me, but I pushed on, telling myself and others that it was my dream job and I wanted to do it well. There were as many downs as ups through this period, but I learned a lot. I have been in the leadership and culture field for over 18 years now. It still gives me a buzz when I see pennies dropping for people, when the so-called 'soft' or 'intangible' work we do leads to positive, concrete outcomes. About six years ago, however, I had my own penny-dropping moment, and it changed how I see myself and started shaping what I'm about to share with you in this book.

Introduction

The penny drops

I was co-facilitating a leadership workshop with a colleague who has the opposite style to me – gregarious, entertaining and loud. He started the workshop and had the group laughing within the first two minutes. I enjoyed his energy until it got closer to my part of the workshop.

As I watched people laughing, the little voice started in my head: 'Gosh, I don't get people laughing so much', 'I'm going to seem boring compared with him', 'What if they disengage?' and 'How am I going to keep the energy up?' The silly thing is, I had been facilitating for over ten years by then and I'd had plenty of positive feedback in the past. I didn't need to worry, but I did.

I stood up and facilitated my part of the workshop until morning tea. Nothing went wrong. People were engaged and ready to take on the rest of the day's learning. At morning tea, however, I felt exhausted. A colleague I had worked with for a few years was participating in the workshop, and she walked over to me during the break. She said, 'Megumi, what's going on? You don't seem your usual self.' I thought to myself, *Oh no, so it was visible to the participants that I had all this internal turmoil?* I told my colleague about my inner voice and how it prevented me from being fully present.

She looked me in the eye and said, 'Megumi, stop comparing yourself with your co-facilitator! You bring something very different to him and that's what makes you valuable. If you keep trying to be like him or keep comparing yourself, we don't get to see the best of you.'

That five-minute interaction was an absolute gem! I got myself back into being present and we had a fantastic workshop. People commented on how much they valued the contrasting styles of the two of us, and that they got a lot out of both.

In retrospect, there had been many hints before this that I needed to appreciate myself and my unique contribution. I was sometimes told not to try so hard to be like someone else or to be overly energetic. I only accepted this intellectually, however, and I didn't know how to fully embrace my own style.

After that penny-dropping moment, though, I began really understanding and appreciating the unique approaches I brought to my work. It was the seed for *Quietly Powerful*.

I started experimenting with reconnecting with my quiet nature and not hiding it. One such experiment was with a client who wanted to hold an all-team strategy review workshop with about 40 people. I designed the workshop so that there were many opportunities for pair, small-group and whole-group discussion. Pre-reading materials as well as questions were sent so that people could reflect before the workshop, should they prefer to do so. And I facilitated the workshop so that most of the talking was done by the client team.

The CEO who commissioned the work gave me feedback afterwards. 'That was a fantastic workshop. People were really engaged; great ideas came out of it and I could see the team taking ownership of the strategy. It was as if you were invisible: you guided us when there was a need, but you had us doing the work, and that made a big difference.'

As I continued to experiment, I kept receiving similar comments about my style, not only in facilitation but also presentations and consulting. The consistent themes that kept coming through were that clients appreciated that I listened and understood their needs, that I ensured that everyone was involved, that my understated style made everyone comfortable to engage, and that my observation skills allowed me to notice and engage the quieter people.

The successes helped me to believe that quietness is valuable and that more people should appreciate and leverage it. And so, in August 2016, I anxiously sent out my first email to a group of contacts, asking whether they or their colleagues would be interested in a breakfast to talk about the challenges of being a quiet professional woman.

Introduction

What is Quietly Powerful?

During its humble beginnings, my business Quietly Powerful was an experiment to see if quieter professional women could benefit from hearing my story. I hosted small breakfasts to share my learnings about why the workplace is challenging for quieter professionals, what holds us back and what we can do about it. The breakfasts kept selling out, so I did many more breakfasts and some learning programs.

When I had reached about 200 women, I noticed that it wasn't just introvert women who were attending. In fact, a few of the women who joined my coaching programs were extroverts. Some of these women were struggling with speaking up and being recognised; others were looking for ways to access their quiet powers.

Two major events convinced me that Quietly Powerful was more than an experiment. The first was a talk at the Vic ICT for Women, a member-based organisation that champions women in STEM (science, technology, engineering and maths) in the Australian state of Victoria. The event sold out a few days before the registration close date, which had not happened before, and on the day, more than 100 people packed the room. Positive feedback comments included, 'one of the best … events I've attended, great topic and speaker' and 'Sorry you had to turn people down, perhaps allow standing room?'

Soon after, men started to approach me and ask why I was 'excluding' them. If my experience as a quieter professional woman was relevant and useful to men, I was happy to share. This led to the second major talk at Ernst & Young, sponsored by both the Asia Professionals Network and Network of Winning Women. Both men and women were invited, and the organisers had chairs and catering organised for about 50 to 70 people, which was their usual turnout. As we opened the doors to the event, though, people just kept coming in; by the time I started the talk, rows of people were standing by the walls and windows, as there were not enough seats. We had about 150 attendees.

By this time, Quietly Powerful had become a movement with the aim of shifting collective beliefs about what good leadership looks, sounds and feels like. I had started researching Quietly Powerful leaders – interviewing people who had successfully progressed in leadership careers using their quieter nature. This research is still continuing, and these interviews have solidified my belief that Quietly Powerful leadership is not only important for giving opportunities to people who feel quietly disempowered, it is important for improving the quality of leadership in organisations and in society. We need Quietly Powerful leaders now more than ever.

A shift in our beliefs about leadership will allow talented quiet professionals to view their quiet nature as a strength and to succeed in their own way, rather than seeing it as a disadvantage. It will also enhance diversity in leadership and help organisations to stop wasting their hidden talent – those quiet achievers that get either overlooked or taken advantage of without recognition. Ultimately, valuing and developing Quietly Powerful leaders and instilling their attributes in not-so-quiet leaders, as well, will address the leadership gap (poor-quality leadership) we are experiencing today.

Quietly Powerful initially drew attention from professionals who are quiet, but now senior organisational leaders, human resources, leadership and talent, diversity and inclusion professionals are seeing how this approach can improve leadership capabilities, gender and cultural diversity, cross-cultural communication, collaboration, and coaching capabilities.

How to use this book

This book challenges quiet professionals to reframe the story they tell themselves about their leadership potential and encourages organisations to expand their ideas about what good leadership looks, sounds and feels like.

Here's a short description of what you will gain from the various chapters:

- **Part I** (Chapters 1–3) describes the organisational and individual cost of undervaluing our quiet nature and quiet approaches to leadership. Most quiet professionals would recognise these challenges, but organisations and not-so-quiet individuals may be surprised to discover the high price of undervaluing their quiet nature.

- **Part II** (Chapters 4–7) offers the reasons why individuals may remain quiet and hidden. It goes beyond introversion, which is often what people talk about. You will find out that being quiet and hidden is a lot more complex and requires further exploration.

- **Part III** (Chapters 8–11) explores why organisations overlook and underutilise their quiet talent. It is an invitation to them to challenge their cognitive and structural biases and to update their thinking on the type of leadership they need and how to get the most out of quiet talent.

- **Part IV** (Chapters 12–17) describes what Quietly Powerful leaders are like, and the quiet superpowers that set them apart as leaders and distinguish them from simply being quiet leaders. Chapters 15 to 17 give individuals the strategies to move from being quietly disempowered to Quietly Powerful.

- **Part V** (Chapters 18–19) invites not-so-quiet people and organisations to also reap the benefits of Quietly Powerful.

My hope is that whether you are quiet or not-so-quiet, you will start to see the power of your quiet nature, so you can use it for your benefit and in your leadership. You might find that you need it more than you realise.

Part I

The quiet wasteland

WE MAY NOT realise it, but there are costs to overlooking quietness and quiet professionals. The first is the obvious waste of talented quiet achievers who feel misunderstood or disempowered. In addition, we may be failing to notice real leaders who could reduce the range of leadership problems we are experiencing today and develop into the leaders we need tomorrow. By not valuing quietness enough, we may also be wasting an opportunity to address serious workplace and societal issues.

Part I will outline the individual, organisational and societal costs of undervaluing quietness and quiet professionals.

Chapter 1

The hidden waste

While I had my own struggles as a quiet Japanese professional woman, I encountered others who were struggling in similar ways, and sometimes worse.

A colleague, who I will call Sally here, worked in a large company as the 'go-to person' for three general managers (GMs) while the company was going through a transformation. The GMs were trying to engage over 100 senior managers to lead the transformation.

When I started to work with her as a change consultant, I saw Sally in action with the GMs as well as the 100-plus senior managers. In her quiet and amiable way, she influenced the way in which the senior managers were engaged and pushed back on the GMs' ideas when she thought they wouldn't work. She presented logical reasons, and the GMs would generally take her advice. The senior managers treated her like a friendly peer, but when Sally asked them to do something, they would do what she asked. And when they had concerns or questions, Sally was usually the first person they spoke to. From what I could see, she was the ultimate influencer and leader with 'soft power', as Yamini Naidu terms it in her book *Power Play*. However, Sally saw herself as a support person to the GMs, someone who did the work in the background.

After I finished my work with Sally, her organisation assessed 200 or so leaders at her level, via an assessment day. The activities included group problem-solving while being observed by assessors, and presenting after 30 minutes' preparation. After the assessment day, each person was debriefed by one of the assessors. I heard that Sally was in tears after the debrief, as she was told that she did not have leadership potential. She went on sabbatical soon after this experience.

Sally was overlooked and misunderstood due to her quieter nature and approach. I was so disappointed to hear this. How could a person's leadership potential be assessed in one day when the role of leadership requires more than a day's work? How could they discount the influential leadership she had demonstrated over months and years?

I have since heard many other stories of talented professionals being overlooked for this reason.

In the early days of Quietly Powerful, I asked over 200 professional women to respond to a survey which asked them whether they felt being quiet was a disadvantage. I remember getting a shock to see that 91 per cent of respondents stated that they often or sometimes felt that they had to behave like an extrovert to get ahead in their careers. In our public breakfast conversations, there were a staggering number of people who felt frustrated that their high-quality work and achievements were overlooked.

The other common experience of quiet professionals is exhaustion from being in noisy work environments where they have to be vocal to be heard or taken seriously. People feel like they have to 'fake it till they make it'. Women are regularly told to do this, and so are quieter men.

One of the depressing aspects of my early days of Quietly Powerful was hearing how quiet professionals had to hide their natural styles and unique talents, as they felt that their quiet nature would hold them back. It was as if they saw their quieter nature as a disadvantage; some even felt that there must be something wrong with them.

This is not only disappointing, but concerning, as a professional in the field of leadership and culture. Firstly, real talent is being wasted because of the bias toward style against substance. Secondly, we are compromising on leadership quality. The best leaders are not being selected due to an outdated mental model of what good leadership looks, sounds and feels like.

Quietness is seen as a weakness

When someone describes a person as 'a bit quiet', what words come to mind?

I've asked this question of hundreds of people in my talks, and the words that commonly come up include 'reserved', 'shy', 'not confident', 'aloof', 'antisocial', 'doesn't contribute', 'passive' and 'meek'. Then a few will share words such as 'considered', 'thoughtful', 'good listener', 'reflective', 'deep thinker' and 'observant'.

The second group of words – which are more complimentary – usually come up after a few of the first group of words have been stated. It is almost as if people remember, 'Oh, that's right, quiet people can be valuable'.

In any case, the word 'powerful' never comes up. Sometimes, in fact, people ask me, 'How can one be quiet *and* powerful?' 'Quietly powerful' is not an idea that is in our collective mindset – yet.

A recruiter once told me of a candidate she put forward to a client who had successfully managed multi-million-dollar projects and was perfect for the role. The candidate completed a psychometric test which indicated he was more on the introvert and agreeable side of the scale, whereupon the hiring manager said he didn't want a 'pussy cat' and decided on another person. The client hiring manager assumed that an introverted and agreeable leader would be too 'soft' and that he wouldn't deliver.

Another senior manager was unsuccessful in obtaining a senior executive role despite being told that he delivered the best strategy presentation out of all the candidates. The feedback from the recruiter who was on the interview panel included, 'Can he step up and go to war?', 'He is too polite' and 'His team is too happy'. It was implied that you need to be dominating and less polite and supportive to be in a senior position.

People may not say this, but some do assume that quieter professionals are not leadership material, or not great speakers, not influential or not engaging. Sometimes quiet professionals are also not seen as confident, which can lead to being perceived as incompetent. What a tragedy, when creative, observant, deep thinkers can be seen like this just because they don't open their mouths as much as others.

Quietness is misunderstood

It's a myth that quiet people are all aloof, not very social and uninterested in other people.

Quiet people don't necessarily dislike people. Many of the Quietly Powerful leaders I interviewed shared how much they enjoy working with people and seeing them grow and thrive. Jane Bird, a quietly spoken senior leader in technology, is one of these. Jane is no geek. Her passion for technology comes from thinking about what technology enables people to do differently. She thrives when working with a team.

Jane shared her experience with me of taking over a team that was rolling out an internally developed software program into supermarkets. Quite a few people had come and gone in the role, and by the time Jane was asked, it was a position no one wanted. She described what it was like:

> *I thought,* Well, it can't get any worse than this, right? *We set about [the work] with the people that had lived through that, the ones that survived, [who had] true resilience and passion for the environment… [W]e created something magnificent. Both in terms of culture and automation, and the relationship with our business customer flourished as a result.*

Jane loved taking on the role, especially with a team which was so diverse. She was the only Australian-born person: the rest were from New Zealand, China, Vietnam, Jersey, England, Delhi. She and members of this team still catch up regularly, 15 years later.

Susan Allen, former Executive General Manager at RACV, never thought of herself as a leader until she was appointed to her first leadership role and realised how she much she enjoyed developing people, and helping them and the organisation to achieve outcomes that she could not on her own. She said:

> *Even though I'm an introvert, I do like spending time with people and finding out about them and their motivations… What do they want to do? What are their goals, and how can I help them get there?*

Being quiet doesn't mean that people are disengaged, either. It may be that they are very engaged and listening actively. They could be thinking deeply about the issues being discussed.

Another myth is that quiet people are not suited to public speaking.

Public speaking is scary for many people, not just quiet professionals. However, it's a skill that can be developed through training and practice. Lisa Evans, Director of Speaking Savvy, has coached many people in public speaking – and she herself is an introvert and shy when not on stage. In her experience, quiet professionals can be excellent speakers. She said:

> *I've discovered in my work that introverts and quieter leaders make excellent public speakers. That's because a lot of the success*

around speaking is in the preparation. Those of us who are quieter – we don't mind staying home and doing all that work. We're [also] very audience-centric, and we really are in tune with those who are in our audience and really understand ... that speaking is all about sharing a message. It's not about me: it's about the audience and what gifts I can share with them through the power of a message. I meet plenty of fellow professional speakers who are introverts, who are quiet, and who absolutely shine on stage.

It's also a myth that you can't influence others if you're quiet.

Most of us associate influence with persuasive speech. If you look closely at people who have influence in the workplace, however, you may notice that there are other approaches to influencing. Paul Boasman, Executive, Financial Strategy & Performance at Telstra, has found that he's able to influence more effectively by speaking with people one at a time or in smaller groups than by speaking to a larger group. His strategy is to share ideas, listen to concerns, ask for their views on what would work, and then incorporate their ideas before taking a concept to the larger group. In most cases, Paul found that this collaborative approach resulted in an endorsement by the time the idea got to the group, rather than him having to persuade the group at that point.

Other examples of influence involve action more than words. Greta Thunberg is a quiet Swedish teenager who decided to organise a school strike to make the point that we need to take more action on the climate crisis. She started protesting outside the Swedish Parliament on her own in August 2018, and by November 2018 a global 'school strike for climate' movement had formed. On 15 March 2019, an estimated 1.4 million students in 112 countries around the world joined her call to strike and protest. Greta has since become a vocal climate activist, speaking in a range of public forums including the World Economic Forum.

In an interview, the young activist said, 'We introverts can make our voices heard'. Greta was inspired by Rosa Parks, an

American activist in the civil rights movement – also a quiet introvert, and best known for her pivotal role in the Montgomery bus boycott. Parks rejected the bus driver's order to relinquish her seat in the 'coloured section' to a white passenger, after the whites-only section was filled. Both Greta Thunberg and Rosa Parks used deliberate action as their influencing tool.

Yamini Naidu, business storyteller, speaker and author, outlines different types of influence tools in her book *Power Play: Game changing influence strategies for leaders*. Yamini shared her thoughts about influencing with me:

> *I often talk about that evolution of influence. So 'hard power' is 'yell and tell'. Hard power, command and control, is very much about rules, about following the rules, and we know now, living in a disruptive world, that just doesn't work anymore. Soft power, which is about collaborating, connecting, consulting, is very much about relationships... if hard power is about rules, soft power is about relationships.*

A related myth is that quiet people cannot sell ideas, services, products or a cause.

If you ask people whether they like being 'sold' an idea, services or a product, most people will say they cringe at the pushy sales approach. The quieter approach to selling involves more listening and less pushing. It's less about the sale, self-promotion or self-interest, and more about helping people with what they're buying, whether it's a product, service or a cause.

Matthew Pollard writes in his book, *The Introvert's Edge: How the quiet and shy can outsell anyone*:

> *Introverts make the best salespeople... when armed with a plan that lets them be their authentic selves. You've been sold a lie: you have to be pushy to be successful in sales. But that's simply not true. You don't have to have the gift-of-the-gab.*

Quiet professionals and leaders are highly effective in many activities but are overlooked due to the stereotypes and myth that they are not. Part of the reason is that they're not 'in your face': they go about their business quietly and don't go telling people how wonderful they are.

Lost in the self-promotion battleground

One of the challenges for quiet professionals in the workplace is the emphasis on self-promotion and the notion that 'Your work does not speak for itself'.

I still remember the first time I wrote an article to post on LinkedIn and to send to my very small newsletter list. I enjoyed the thinking and writing part, then when it was time to post it, I froze. I read and re-read the article ten times. I sent it to my husband and a few friends asking for feedback. After incorporating the feedback, I re-read and edited it a few more times. I worried about what comments I might receive. Before I knew it, days had passed and I still hadn't posted the article. Friday afternoon arrived, and I told myself that if I didn't post it that week, I would never do it. My heart was in my mouth as I placed the mouse cursor on the 'Publish' button. It was 4:49 pm; I pressed the button and I closed my eyes. When I opened them, nothing bad had happened! Millions of people post articles every day. While I knew that, my first time felt as if I was about to jump out of a plane!

As an independent consultant, speaker and author, I am regularly reminded of the need to promote myself and my business. However, whenever I think about promoting myself, my business or my programs, I find myself attacked by a barrage of inner criticisms such as 'You're showing off', 'Who are you to promote how good you are?' and 'What do you know that others don't know?' The only way I get over this is to tell myself that I am sharing useful information to help people, and that if I don't share, I'm letting people down. It has gotten easier over time, but I still find that I have to put my brain into a different gear to do marketing and promotion work. It feels very different to when I am doing what I love: the creative work of thinking and writing.

So, when people tell me that they loathe self-promotion, I totally get it. It feels like attention-seeking and that feels foreign and uncomfortable for quiet professionals. Being told to self-promote regularly is like being told to play your least favourite music because it's good for you. You can do it if you have to, reluctantly, but it doesn't *feel* like it's good for you, and you probably want to run away from it. The worst part is that the music will stay in your head, even if you do move away!

Quiet professionals are regularly told to be more visible, speak up more and work on their personal brand. Many women are sent to women's leadership programs to improve in these areas and given tips on looking confident and powerful. Quiet professionals often find this frustrating, and at times feel at a loss when their talent, good work and solid results are not recognised and others who are good self-promoters do get recognised. It feels like organisations value style over substance. (More on this issue in Part III of the book.)

Often, quiet professionals give up before they even begin, by saying that they're 'not good at self-promoting'. Most of these people have not been given the strategies or tools to help them to be visible without feeling like they are bragging or being fake.

How much talent is wasted in your organisation? In the environment of talent shortage and needing better quality leadership, organisations which find and develop this hidden talent will have an advantage over others.

Chapter 2

Leadership gap

We have a leadership gap at organisational, political and social levels and I would not be the first to point this out.

In a *Harvard Business Review (HBR)* article, 'Do you hate your boss?', Manfred F.R. Kets de Vries shares a global survey which revealed that 70 per cent of employees are not engaged at work and did not have anything nice to say about their bosses. In another *HBR* article, 'Talent management: Boards give their companies an "F"', Boris Groysberg and Deborah Bell indicated that fewer than 20 per cent of boards are confident that their organisations have a grip on their leadership problems. Gallup research reports that companies fail to choose the candidate with the right management talent for the job a staggering 82 per cent of the time. When managers account for a 70 per cent variance in employee engagement scores and study after study shows that engagement impacts productivity, turnover and profitability, quality of leadership is not a 'soft' issue.

It's common to hear people complaining about their bosses and how they are impacting their ability to perform at their best.

We find *Dilbert* cartoons and comedy shows like *The Office* funny because they are sometimes not far from reality.

That's not to say there aren't any good leaders out there, but we hear of too many stories about leadership failures, despite billions of dollars being invested in leadership development. Poor leadership is showing up at organisational, political and social levels, locally and globally. We should therefore ask ourselves:

- Are we selecting the right type of people for leadership positions?
- Are we developing the right mindsets, skills and behaviours in our leaders?

Dr Tomas Chamorro-Premuzic, author of *Why Do So Many Incompetent Men Become Leaders? (and how to fix it)* has raised this question from a gender perspective, but with an underlying assertion that we are selecting the wrong type of people for leadership positions. He claims that 'we should not lower our standards when we select women, but we should raise them when we select men'. He is critical of how organisations overvalue the appearance of confidence and charisma.

My research has involved interviewing a range of people to find out what makes them effective as leaders – including Quietly Powerful leaders, CEOs, company directors, entrepreneurs, consultants, HR, leadership, talent, recruitment and diversity and inclusion professionals. The research reveals the differences between the traits commonly associated with people being selected for leadership positions and those that make leaders effective.

The rest of this chapter explores several leadership issues we face today that could be addressed by having Quietly Powerful leadership, regardless of personality.

Ego, greed and self-interest-driven leadership

Leadership driven by ego, greed and self-interest is costly and dangerous. More and more examples have been surfacing of leadership failures due to greed and self-interest taking over. The Australian Banking Royal Commission has publicly highlighted the symptoms of self-interest-driven cultures developing in organisations. The 'Final Report of the Royal Commission into Misconduct in the Banking, Superannuation and Financial Services Industry' states:

> *In almost every case, the conduct in issue was driven not only by the relevant entity's pursuit of profit but also by individuals' pursuit of gain, whether in the form of remuneration for the individual or profit for the individual's business. Providing a service to customers was relegated to second place. Sales became all important.*

While I am sure there were individuals in these organisations who stood up against what was going on, many consciously or unconsciously allowed it to continue. Whether it was deliberate on the part of the individuals involved or not, the perception is that leaders have created environments in which employees put achieving their bonuses for reaching profit targets before their customers and ethics.

There's a growing list of examples of appalling misuse of power: abuse of corporate or public funds, misleading customers and shareholders, under-payment of staff, abuse of privacy, environmental abuse, toxic cultures, bullying and harassment. These cases are not limited to the for-profit organisations, either: such behaviour has been seen in the public service and in government, religious, educational and other institutions.

The Royal Commission into Institutional Responses to Child Sexual Abuse outlined lessons such as:

Children are more likely to be sexually abused in institutional contexts where the community has an unquestioning respect for the authority of the institution.

Leadership and organisational culture can include risk factors such as the failure to listen to children or prioritising the reputation of an institution over the safety and wellbeing of children.

The Commission highlighted the high price of not questioning authority and allowing self-interested leaders to remain in positions of power. While many of these cases have been made visible by whistleblowers, corporate collapses, Royal Commissions and public outcry (such as the #metoo movement), many remain unspoken about and unaddressed.

Stanford professor Robert Sutton, author of *The A--hole Survival Guide: How to deal with people who treat you like dirt*, talks about the hundreds of studies detailing how power can change the way people treat others. 'They're less focused on their needs, less good at stifling their own impulses and they see other people more as objects toward an end,' he said.

Similarly, in *The Power Paradox: How we gain and lose influence*, Dr Dacher Keltner refers to many studies that show how power changes behaviour. His and others' research have shown that people with power tend to act out of self-interest and more like 'sociopaths'. He writes that 'people with power tend to behave like patients who have damaged their brain's orbitofrontal lobes, a condition that seems to cause overly impulsive and insensitive behaviour.'

Wharton Professor of Psychology Adam Grant, on the other hand, interviewed two dozen leaders (including the current or former CEOs of Microsoft, Google, General Motors, Goldman Sachs and the Gates Foundation) and concluded, 'Power doesn't corrupt. It just exposes who leaders really are'. So, when you promote leaders who prioritise self-interest, who like to be in charge and have power over others, these characteristics will be amplified and cause many of the problems we see in leadership today.

Quietly Powerful leaders are less focused on themselves and more focused on the work, the organisation, the team and the bigger mission. Their natural approach is not to 'power over' people but to share their power to achieve the mission. When being of service is the motivator for taking leadership positions, leaders are less likely to be corrupted by power, as self-interest is secondary.

The extent to which organisations can get away with self-interested leadership is diminishing and reputational damage is severe. Strategy&, the consulting arm of PwC, released a survey in 2018 showing that the rate of CEO turnover at the world's largest 2,500 companies has reached 17.5 per cent, the highest since the survey started in 2000. A decade earlier, less than a tenth of expulsions were triggered by ethical lapses, while in 2018, this figure was 39 per cent. Ethical lapses include fraud, bribery, insider trading, environmental disasters, inflated résumés and sexual indiscretions. It's not that more CEOs are behaving less ethically, it's that there has been a shift in standards and expectations of organisations and senior leadership.

Given the cost and dangers of ego, greed and self-interest-driven leadership, organisations need to find and develop leaders who are less likely to be corrupted by power.

Leaders can't know everything

Our world is increasingly complex; disruption is now the key threat and opportunity for organisations. Whether it's via technology, business model transformation or other ways we may not even be aware of yet, innovative entrepreneurs and organisations are changing the rules of the game.

In such an uncertain, complex and inter-connected world, it is impossible for one leader or a few leaders to know or predict anything. The all-knowing leader with a clear vision may be right from time to time, but it is becoming harder to pull off. They are less likely to succeed, as it is impossible for one person to know what is really happening or be creative enough to respond. Leaders who dominate conversations and fail to listen to and consider ideas from a variety of people – including those who may disagree with them – will make uninformed choices and limit creative thinking.

Elizabeth Proust, an experienced board executive and former Chairman of the Australian Institute of Company Directors, said that companies without diversity in boards will be left behind in this changing, disruptive world:

> *As we see companies move to genuine diversity of women, people of different backgrounds and different thinking styles – looking beyond the traditional former CEOs and former professional services to people with marketing skills, digital skills, strategic skills – then you're seeing boards constituted quite differently. Given everything that's happening with AI, with the digital space and with disruption in every industry, if boards aren't thinking, not just of what they need today to meet the competition, but what they'll need in the future, then they'll be overtaken.*

Boards, leadership teams and organisations that draw on the expertise of a range of people – including people who may not appear to 'fit' – increase their chances of success.

Hal Gregersen, Executive Director of MIT's Leadership Center, explained in 'Being Quiet Is Part of Being a Good CEO' how easily leaders become insulated from information they need and how this can lead to a plethora of unexpected problems. Whether it's when a leader arrives into a new company, or when a leader needs to create transformational change or create an environment for cutting-edge innovation, the most successful leaders asked different questions in order to get new answers to problems. The CEOs who asked better questions and spoke out about what they didn't know were the ones who obsessed about the customers and their experience of their organisations.

Listening from the place of not knowing is a powerful yet undervalued leadership skill, critically important in the VUCA (volatile, uncertain, complex, ambiguous) world. As Diana Renner and Steven D'Souza say in their book, *Not Knowing*, 'the ability to question as a matter of habit, to admit that the lens through which we are looking at the world is subjective and flawed, is an essential leadership skill'. In organisations, most people are valued and rewarded for their expertise and knowledge and their ability to give quick, smart answers. In complex environments, this tendency to have all the answers can become a weakness.

Quietly Powerful leaders are comfortable enough in themselves to know that they don't know everything. They rely on and listen to others' expertise and perspectives. They create the space for others' ideas to be heard and considered. Their decisions are thoughtful, made after they have considered multiple perspectives and the complexity of the issue.

Elizabeth Proust, in her Chairman and Board member roles in large organisations, uses her strength in listening, reflection and openness to step back and consider the consequences of critical decisions in complex situations. In our interview, she said:

> *Reflection – both self-reflection [and] reflection on the dynamics in the team – and not making a fast decision on important issues are strengths of quieter leaders. Especially when what you are facing is a complex situation: then the quieter, more reflective people can say, 'Can we just step back and think about the consequences of the decision?' I think one of my strengths is… being open to having my mind changed and saying why.*

Leaders who can gather intelligence and generate creative ideas from a variety of sources, who can listen and be influenced by them and then make decisions, are far more likely to make informed, wiser choices. In addition, they are more likely to develop proactive people who want to contribute their expertise and creativity.

Simon Harrington, during his time in senior leadership roles in the Royal Australian Navy, found that complex decisions required input from a range of experts. Contrary to the view of the stereotypical military leader, he said that quiet leaders were able to listen more effectively to make more informed decisions:

If you're commanding a ship, you can only have one person manoeuvring the ship at any time. If you have two people giving different orders, confusion reigns and that's when real trouble starts... But to get to that position in a complex operation, you have to do an awful lot of planning, and you need to talk to all the experts... and you need to make sure that you have input from everyone who's relevant.

Simon continued to reflect on his experiences and shared that quiet leaders were more effective because they listen and take into account everything that's going on:

They're not so busy blowing their own trumpet or making a noise, so to speak. And life is getting more and more complex: that means you need more subject matter experts to make sure that everything is taken into account, or as much as possible, and that requires listening and allowing the subject matter experts to have their say.

He believes that more and more teamwork is going to be required, because one person can't know everything about a topic. So, leaders will need to bring out the best in all the people in the team.

How often do you encounter leaders who have the level of humility needed to acknowledge that they don't know something, leaders who take time to listen to a range of people – regardless of rank – and think through what they have heard, who are willing to be challenged and open to changing their thinking? How often do you find leaders who are comfortable with uncertainty and willing to experiment, fail and adapt?

Simplistic and quick decision-making

For organisations facing complex issues, simplistic and quick decision-making can make problems worse.

In 1958, American scientist Ancel Keys conducted a study called the Seven Countries Study, which examined the link between diet and cardiovascular disease. Keys revealed that the countries where fat consumption was the highest had a high rate of disease, supporting the idea that dietary fat caused heart disease. The problem was that he left out countries where fat consumption was high but heart disease was low, such as Holland and Norway, and countries where fat consumption was low but the rate of heart disease was high, such as Chile.

In 1977, an American committee of the US senate led by George McGovern published the first 'Dietary Goals for the United States' in order to reverse the epidemic of heart disease in the country. The key message was to eat less fat and cholesterol. These guidelines received major criticism at the time from many respected scientists like John Yudkin (who insisted that sugar was to blame) and the American Medical Association. However, publishing the 'American Dietary Guidelines' was considered an achievement for the American Government and ideas to the contrary were ignored or silenced.

This marked the beginning of the obsession with low-fat diets, based on the simple assumption of flawed research findings. People started to believe that eating fat made us fat, such that high-fat foods like butter, full-cream milk and egg yolks were avoided, and supermarkets started filling up with low-fat foods, many of them processed and with a high sugar content. For most people, this felt intuitively correct and our cognitive biases were left unchecked.

Professor John Yudkin's book *Pure, White and Deadly*, written in 1972, warned against sugar and only became widely acknowledged in 2009 when Dr Robert Lustig, Professor of Paediatric

Endocrinology at the University of California, delivered a lecture called 'Sugar: the Bitter Truth'. It was posted on YouTube and had received over 8.2 million hits at the time of writing.

Data shows that the obesity epidemic started around the time these dietary guidelines were published and the type 2 diabetes epidemic followed soon after, particularly in countries that embraced the low-fat mantra. After more recent research, scientists and medical doctors now blame this low-fat obsession for triggering the multitude of health problems we face today. While there is still debate about the impact of sugar versus fat, the simplistic view that saturated fat alone was to blame has caused more problems than it has solved. The human body is too complex: eliminating one element can have all kinds of unintended consequences.

While I am in no way qualified to comment on the dietary guidelines, this example demonstrates the huge cost of simplistic solutions to complex problems.

How often have you been frustrated by someone's tendency to over-simplify complex issues or the solutions to them? When leaders buy into this approach, we end up with a list of quick wins and band-aid solutions to perhaps slow the ship from sinking – but the ship is sinking, nonetheless. Everyone is busy, with a to-do list that keeps growing.

In his book *How to Lead a Quest*, Dr Jason Fox calls this 'delusions of progress'. It's when we get hooked on a sense of progress and feeling that we're being productive by doing 'busy work' which may not necessarily contribute to real, meaningful progress. Ron Heifetz and Marty Linsky's book *The Practice of Adaptive Leadership* also cautions against applying simple technical solutions based on past knowledge to complex adaptive problems.

One of the greatest dangers of simplistic approaches and rushed decision-making is how we can be misled by our cognitive biases. Nobel Prize–winning behavioural economist and author of *Thinking, Fast and Slow*, Daniel Kahneman, cautions against using gut-based decision-making too early, particularly for strategic and critical decisions.

Unfortunately, the desire to look like we've achieved something and made progress pushes us further into short-term and simple solutions. Whatever is difficult or too complex and ambiguous gets put on the backburner.

When operating in a VUCA environment, over-simplification, quick decision-making, and solutions based on past knowledge may risk an organisation's success or even survival. The Royal Banking Commission commented on 'band-aid solutions' and short-term focus as two of the causes of the issues raised. More considered approaches taken by Quietly Powerful leaders can sometimes be labelled as slow or indecisive; however, in the complex situations we face today, we need this patience and thoughtfulness.

Cultural complexity

Clive Peter spoke of a time when he worked at Ford developing capability in the Asia Pacific region. One of his favourite experiences was working in Thailand with a group of people from different cultures, including Thai nationals, an engineering team from Japan, a design team from the USA and three Australians:

> *I was trying to navigate between all three groups to get a successful outcome… There were a lot of lessons learned at the start, particularly around when 'yes' means 'yes', or when 'yes' means 'no', depending on the culture. It was important to listen carefully, not only to words and language, but to body language as well. I would attribute our success to being able to listen, to adapt, to understand how to share your goals and listen respectfully, while still driving for an outcome.*

Organisations are increasingly multi-cultural, with employees, clients, suppliers and partners from around the globe. For organisations to survive, grow and thrive in the world of globalisation, we cannot ignore the need to work across differences.

Multi-national organisations and organisations expanding or outsourcing offshore have experienced this multi-culturalism, sometimes resulting in great difficulty. Different cultures bring different perspectives and ways of operating and interacting, often adding layers of complexity. At its worst, it is a source of miscommunication, misunderstandings, frustrations and conflict. At its best, it expands our thinking, allows us to reach more markets and enriches our own experience and development.

In her book *A World of Difference*, Felicity Menzies makes a case for cultural intelligence succeeding in the globalised market. She refers to her own experiences as well as to research such as a 2015 McKinsey study which makes a compelling case for ethnic diversity at board and top management levels. However, she also highlights a large gap referred to in the 'IBM Global Chief Executive Officer Study' – in that more than half the businesses did not feel they were flexible enough to respond to change across diverse markets.

In working across cultures, it is essential to apply the advice of the late Stephen Covey: 'Seek first to understand before you are understood'. There is a real risk of dysfunction when leaders have mindsets of 'I know it all', 'I'm right, you're wrong' or 'different = wrong', and this results in telling and not asking. Dominant, outspoken, overconfident or narcissistic leaders who do not adapt add significant risks to these complex relationships and ultimately the organisation's success.

Quietly Powerful leaders will typically spend more time listening and observing in order to understand before communicating or taking action. They allow space for others to share their way of working. Their humility is often received with respect and this speeds up trust-building.

Poor listening = low trust

Time and time again I hear people in organisations say they wish their leaders would listen to them more. The desire to be heard is strong, particularly when you have people in the organisation who care about the work, are proactive and want to contribute their best. For these people to feel like they are not heard has a devastating effect on their trust and engagement.

> *The biggest concern for any organization should be when their most passionate people become quiet.*
> —Tim McClure

Organisations can also damage trust by not listening to customer concerns. When societal concerns are ignored, that's when you end up with the likes of a Royal Commission. Even if the concerns cannot be addressed immediately, listening and acknowledging the issue is what most people need. At every level – individual all the way to societal – listening is the most under-utilised trust-building tool.

Mark Lowy specialises in turning around projects in trouble. His quiet style enables him to listen such that sponsors and stakeholders feel heard and understood. They start working with Mark because they understand that he is on their side:

> *So often, I do less of the talking and more of the listening. It's about empathy and understanding. What you're doing is that you're building a level of trust… My experience in meetings where you've got a leader or a project manager who tends to dominate the conversation, a lot of people will walk away from that meeting going, 'Well, he doesn't know what he's talking about', or, 'I don't want to work for this guy or woman'.*

Mark consistently found that by investing in listening and building trust upfront, people were more willing to work alongside him, and the investment paid off in the form of faster and better outcomes or turnarounds, and positive working relationships. He found that people would go the extra mile because they had been heard and solid relationships had been built.

Similarly, Clive Peter – having worked in a number of multi-national organisations – believes that when starting with a new team or organisation, listening is key to building trust. Sometimes having too much energy and drive to impress can backfire. He said:

> *If you are new to an organisation or trying to implement something that is new, I think running too fast at the start can be problematic. It would be better to share the goal or the objective clearly to people in a respectful way and then listen, because most people can be fearful of change, whether it's at a conscious level or at an unconscious level. When people are allowed to speak and have been heard, they become much more open to exploring alternatives and to working with you to be aligned around a goal.*

Helen Macfarlane, Partner at Addisons, also builds connections and trust with clients through listening and observing:

> *In terms of dealing with clients, it can be noticing what's said and what's not said, observing body language. When someone is doing all the talking and needs the limelight or the attention, they focus on themselves… Particularly in the legal profession, our clients expect us to partner and collaborate with them, and so they want it to be about them, working with them.*

How would you feel working for a leader who listens to you, who asks questions in order to understand, who is happy to collaborate and gives credit to the team and others? How would you feel working with a leader who allows others to take the lead and is more focused on the work than themselves?

I would most likely contribute my best. Wouldn't you?

Listening not only allows leaders to make informed decisions, listening builds trust.

All talk and no results

At the Quietly Powerful talks, I ask people to stand if they have been frustrated with 'smooth-talkers' who seem to get ahead regardless of their competence or ability to deliver results. Usually, about 70 to 90 per cent of the group stand up. They have seen these polished presentations and great promises turn to nothing. We are disappointed in leaders who turn out to be all talk and no results. Of course, there may be valid reasons for the non-delivery. However, can organisations afford to continue this pattern of rewarding those with style but insufficient substance?

Clive Peter believes that we are overly influenced by current marketing, which tends to focus us on a grand inspirational leader as opposed to the contributions of all who have. On the flipside, he believes that:

> *Quiet leadership allows everyone to be successful. I actually think you have much more 'small P' power… the ability to affect change or accomplishment when you lead quietly. It also allows you to enjoy leading a lot more because you allow other people to occupy the space. That's a very enabling thing to do. I think the more people who occupy more leadership space, the higher you can rise.*

Helen Macfarlane found it challenging earlier in her career, as a quiet lawyer who was expected to speak up and promote herself. However, she has seen change as clients became more diverse, with more women and people from culturally diverse backgrounds in senior decision-making roles:

> *People these days, they'll still be entertained by the extrovert with the great jokes and the showmanship, but… some people, they prefer one-on-one contact… it's not about me and the show… or how doing work for you is good for my ego. It's about how I can help you.*

It may seem that Quietly Powerful leaders do not sell themselves, but they are often the ones who focus on the client and deliver. It seems absurd that these quiet achievers are told to promote themselves when they spend their precious time on delivering results. Certainly, they should share their achievements and learnings, but overemphasis on visibility and self-promotion above delivery reinforces the bias for style against substance.

This unconscious bias has serious consequences for innovation and engagement, as the best ideas are not always heard and it disengages people who have something valuable to contribute. Do organisations need people who deliver results or people who talk eloquently about delivering results? Who gets listened to more in your organisation?

Centralised leadership

Many organisations say they want people to 'step up' and show leadership at every level. Unfortunately, dominating leaders can take up too much space, such that people around them are unable to step up. If you see people in an organisation looking to the positional leaders to make most decisions or simply going along with the positional leaders' ideas, you have a problem.

I'm regularly told by senior managers that middle management do not step up enough. Some organisations talk about 'permafrost', implying that middle managers are frozen in the ice ages or that communication gets stuck in the ice layer. When you speak with the middle managers, though, you will often hear that the senior leaders are not listening or understanding how to get the best out of them. It would be easy to blame the middle managers for not stepping up or the senior managers for not making space, but blaming doesn't solve the issue.

It is risky for organisations to create dependencies on one or a small number of leaders at the top. When people are overly reliant on the positional leader to solve problems, make decisions and take charge, the organisation is easily destabilised by the leaders' absence. This also reinforces a low accountability culture where fingers are pointed upwards, especially when things go wrong.

Quietly Powerful leaders create space for people to step into leadership. They prefer not to be the centre of attention, so sharing power and consulting people to gain input from all levels often comes naturally. They enable teams to take the lead where they have strengths.

Steve Hodgkinson, who has held numerous leadership positions and is now CIO at Victorian Health and Human Services, said that a big part of his leadership approach was getting out of the team's way and empowering people:

Keeping out of people's way is an acknowledgement that I don't know everything. It's not like I know all the answers, or I even know anything about some of the things we're dealing with – I need people that I can trust who do. And so why would I [get] in their way? What I need to do is work out what I can do to help.

Similarly, Clive Peter, now Manager, People and Culture at the City of Melbourne, told me that his primary leadership approach is one of enabling:

I like to surround myself with good, competent people who have shared values. I try and lead from behind as the servant leader. If you're a good leader, your leadership is the sum total of your team, it's not the sum total of you. I think the further up in an organisation you go, [the more] it's a mistake to believe that you alone are making that tremendous difference. You enable people to make a tremendous difference and I think that's the value you add as a leader.

This distributed leadership makes the team and organisation more resilient. Because Quietly Powerful leaders are comfortable with themselves, they are not threatened by others' success and they love seeing others thrive and succeed.

Simon Harrington shared that letting people do their jobs and lead their part is critical to successful leadership in the military, where leaders are expected to develop people. He said:

You've got to let people get on and do their jobs. If they've got a task, you let them do it. It is important to let people learn and make mistakes. You learn much more from making a mistake than you do from getting things right... If you step in before the mistake is made, you deny that person a learning opportunity... If I did step in, at the end of it I'd say, 'Look, I had to step in then, because you were going to run the ship aground. I could see it coming and I wasn't convinced you could, or that you knew how to get yourself out of the situation'.

Wharton University's organisational psychology professor Adam Grant (along with co-authors Francesca Gino of Harvard Business School and David Hofmann of the University of North Carolina's Kenan-Flagler Business School) has shared research on the power of introverted leaders. The study shows that, 'When employees are proactive, introverted managers lead them to earn higher profits. When employees are not proactive, extraverted managers lead them to higher profits'. While the study explains how higher performance is achieved when proactive employees are paired with introvert-style leaders, it begs the chicken and egg question: do introvert-style leaders enable employees to become more proactive while extrovert-style leaders cause employees to become less proactive?

If you want proactive teams from which leaders emerge at every level, the answer may be to find and develop quieter leaders who will give them the space.

Attracting and retaining diverse talent

It is more critical than ever before to attract, retain and engage diverse talent.

While organisations can pay more and offer attractive conditions, organisational leaders and culture also have a significant, if not greater, influence on talent attraction and retention. According to Gallup's 'State of the American Manager' report, 'Managers account for at least 70 per cent of the variance in employee engagement scores'. As the saying goes, people don't leave organisations, they leave their managers.

Diversity and inclusion are not just about tapping into a larger pool of available talent. They are also about getting the most out of the diverse range of people you have hired. Being inclusive is a hallmark of good leadership and organisational culture. Gallup research found that employees' perceptions of inclusivity were that someone 'cares about me as a person' and 'my opinions seem to count'. They also found that engaged employees are more likely to say their company values diverse ideas. As such, inclusive leadership is a much broader issue than diversity and inclusion – it is an organisational leadership, culture, engagement and performance issue. Inclusive culture and leadership are critical advantages, especially in fields experiencing talent shortages, such as technology, science, engineering and growing fields such as cybersecurity.

Quietly Powerful leaders are naturally inclusive due to their observation skills and curiosity to find talent where others may have overlooked it. By taking the time to listen, observe and ask, they are more likely to understand and appreciate someone's unique strengths – even hidden talents – and how they can contribute to the team and organisation. In addition, their humility often leads them to step back to allow other people to contribute their knowledge, expertise and talents. Quietly Powerful leaders can be mentors who instil self-belief, inspiring the minority who may have been marginalised.

Giovanni Stagno made listening and observing his top priority upon returning to Ernst & Young's Australian practice, after spending ten years working for the company in Japan. He ensured he listened to everyone's stories of what mattered most to them, regardless of rank, in order to genuinely understand their position in the business. He carefully observed their behavioural patterns to inform his decisions on the best methods of influencing and managing the business. The effectiveness of this approach came to light during a positive 360-degree feedback process 18 months later:

> *People felt very good about the fact that I was genuine in listening and taking feedback and ideas regardless of that person's rank within the team. That was key in effectively leading. The fact that people could say what they wanted [meant that they] walked away knowing they were heard.*

Helen Macfarlane is also driven by recognising people's efforts and achievements, particularly the quiet achievers. She said:

> *When I work with my team, it's very important for me to recognise the hard work [and] the achievements of those members, particularly if they're quiet achievers themselves... you need to promote everybody that's part of your team. I have a special soft spot for the quiet achievers, because I know from experience it can be a struggle.*

If you want inclusive cultures and leaders in your organisation, finding and promoting Quietly Powerful leaders could be the solution.

~

We are faced with unprecedented challenges in organisations and in the world such that we cannot ignore the current leadership gap. As one LinkedIn contributor said:

> *By not paying attention to quietly powerful people we rob ourselves of a significant opportunity to improve leadership in companies. As the Royal Commission into Misconduct in the*

Banking, Superannuation and Financial Services Industry is showing, we sorely need this improvement.

Organisations are not only wasting quiet talent, they are missing out on the opportunity to close the leadership gap. As an organisation, do you need to lift the quality of your leadership? Do you need a more proactive, collaborative and creative culture? Do you want faster progress on diversity and inclusion? Finding and developing Quietly Powerful leaders is one solution that has been overlooked.

Chapter 3

Personal damage

Not only are we wasting quiet talent and not closing the leadership gap, we are also doing damage to ourselves by not valuing our quiet nature.

'Covering' – not being able to be authentic

In 2013, I began developing my own ideas about Quietly Powerful. I spoke with my wonderful extrovert colleague and friend Sonia as we were driving home from co-facilitating a workshop. I shared my penny-dropping moment with her about how much I was affected by my inner critic, and how my colleague in the audience had noticed this and told me to value my own style.

We reminisced about the facilitator training we had done together and how our teacher used to tell me that I was putting on a 'professional' face and not being authentic. It was a struggle for me to find my own style and be myself, partly because I was so used to putting on the 'professional' face, but also because I hadn't seen quieter role models in the leadership facilitation field.

I didn't know how to be authentic and effective until I started to experiment.

When I began to share my ideas of Quietly Powerful with Sonia, I started to stumble over my words and felt embarrassed. My inner voices were to taking over again: 'Why would you want to admit to people that you are a quiet professional who struggled to be heard?', 'You will lose credibility as a leadership facilitator and consultant', 'Why should anyone listen to you, when people like Susan Cain have already spoken about it to the world?'

It was lucky that Sonia was listening intently to me. She thought it was a great idea and told me that I had to do it. If it weren't for her encouragement, my inner voices would have talked me out of it.

It is amazing how difficult it was to own up to my own authenticity. I thought my quiet side was flawed and something to hide, especially in a work context. I noticed that I felt somewhat embarrassed when I admitted to being a quiet professional.

'Covering' – when we feel we cannot be authentic, when we feel we have to hide parts of ourselves to fit into the mainstream – is detrimental to our sense of self. Kenji Yoshino, who writes and speaks about covering, found that '60 to 73 per cent of individuals, depending on the particular axis of covering that we looked at, said that this was somewhat to extremely detrimental to their sense of self'.

How can we ever be authentic if we don't appreciate our quiet nature?

Burnout, anxiety and mental health

One of my coaching clients – let's call her Tara – came to see me because she was an extrovert and wanted to learn to access her quieter side. She was well known as an outgoing, social and energetic person, but she was getting increasingly tired of others' expectations that she would be that way. She was tired of her friends and colleagues asking her what was wrong when she was quieter or didn't show up to gatherings.

When we started our coaching, Tara was working in a toxic environment with a difficult boss. She was overworked and suffered 'performance punishment', where she was given more to do because she was someone who delivered. Over time, her energy and passion for the work diminished, as she felt like she was being used, and the toxic relationships caused her stress. Tara was burned out, but despite her exhaustion, she was still expected to be the extroverted person who brought energy to gatherings. She didn't know how to say no to invitations or how to find space for herself.

Tara started meditation and yoga and worked on being more mindful of her thoughts. She learned to say no to more invitations, to stop being the social coordinator all the time and to manage her thoughts about letting others down and the fear of missing out. With more space for self-reflection about what she really wanted in her career and life, she was able to achieve clarity about the type of roles she wanted to apply for. Tara was soon able to get a new job that made her happier and where she was able to maintain space for herself.

The World Health Organization now officially recognises burnout in the 'International Classification of Diseases and Related Health Problems'. It is described as 'a syndrome conceptualized as resulting from chronic workplace stress that has not been successfully managed'. It is characterised by three key factors: 'feelings of energy depletion or exhaustion; increased mental distance from one's job, or feelings of negativism or cynicism related to one's job; and reduced professional efficacy'.

Whichever study you look at, statistics and trends on burnout and mental health issues are bleak.

A 2018 Gallup study of nearly 7,500 full-time employees found that 23 per cent of employees reported feeling burned out at work very often or always, while an additional 44 per cent reported feeling burned out sometimes.

A 2018 review by a team of 28 global experts was published in *The Lancet* medical journal, estimating that the cost of the (mental health) crisis will hit US$16 trillion by 2030. According to the World Health Organization, depression is the third leading cause of illness and disability among adolescents, and suicide is the third leading cause of death in teenagers between 15 and 19.

Studies on human physiology show that noise has a physical, stress-inducing effect. In his article 'This is Your Brain on Silence' (*Nautilus*, 7 July 2016), science journalist Daniel A. Gross shares:

> *Neurophysiological research suggests that noises first activate the amygdalae, clusters of neurons located in the temporal lobes of the brain, associated with memory formation and emotion. This activation prompts an immediate release of stress hormones like cortisol. People who live in consistently loud environments often experience chronically elevated levels of stress hormones.*

Some of us intuitively know this already, which is why we pay hundreds of dollars for noise-cancelling headphones and weekends away in nature, and hundreds and thousands of dollars for silent meditation courses.

Dr Jenny Brockis, medical doctor and specialist in brain health and high-performance thinking, said:

> *It's vitally important for people to recognise that, no matter if you're the most extroverted person on the planet or the most introverted, we all benefit from allocating time to find that quiet space to just be and to think on our own. As our lives become increasingly busy and we continue to integrate with our new technologies, taking time out to be still is essential to manage our growing mental load, reduce stress and remind ourselves we are human.*

Personal damage

The problem is, without the headphones and when you come back from the retreats, you are right back in the noisy, stress-inducing state. Our inability to access our inner quiet, calm state reduces our ability to handle stress and anxiety.

Significant amounts of scientific evidence from the last 40 or so years show that meditation or training of the mind has a positive effect on wellbeing, with improved mental health and workplace performance as a result.

In their 2016 article 'Mindfulness, Behaviour Change and Decision Making: An experimental trial', Jessica Pykett et al. wrote:

> *Research studies in workplaces have primarily emphasised the role of mindfulness programmes on staff wellbeing, mental health and stress-reduction – tackling problems of sickness absence, presenteeism, high staff turnover, depression and anxiety.*
>
> *… Research and commentary has also explored the business role of mindfulness in terms of improving employee performance, resilience and social relationships in the workplace, work engagement and in reducing emotional exhaustion and improving job satisfaction.*

Yet, despite all the evidence, meditation and mindfulness training are still perceived as unscientific, spiritual, or not for the workplace, and are not taken as seriously as, say, sales and presentation training. There appears to be a pattern: skills that are visible and action-based are valued, those that are quiet and internally based are undervalued. With mental health becoming one of the biggest and growing health issues of our time, training our minds is no longer just a nice thing to do.

It is somewhat ironic that most working people look forward to some peace and quiet in their holidays and will pay for a retreat or a digital detox to access their quiet nature. It would be less costly and more sustainable if we valued and accessed our quiet nature more regularly, to avoid burnout and maintain our mental wellbeing.

Loneliness

The 2018 'Australian Loneliness Report' revealed that one in four Australians reported feeling lonely each week. The report claims that 'Loneliness is a growing concern globally, because of its reported impact on health and wellbeing'.

A number of initiatives exist to address the loneliness epidemic, such as:

- **Men's Shed** – a place for men to come together and build and repair items for the community while building connections

- **Gather My Crew** – a free online rostering tool that helps families, friends and community members organise themselves in support of someone who needs help

- **Positive Connect** – a strengths-based group therapy program provided by Melbourne's Swinburne University of Technology, intended to assist young people who are experiencing psychosis and social anxiety to build their social interaction skills.

There are also many interest-based social groups and traditional clubs and membership organisations that support social connections.

These initiatives are important, particularly for people who are disconnected and isolated for a range of reasons. The one query I do have, however, is whether the strongly held common belief that humans are social creatures may have exacerbated the feeling of loneliness in some. This belief implies that if you are not with others, there's something wrong with you, and you are missing out on what normal humans 'should' want. We are overselling the human need for social connection and underselling the need for solitude.

From the outside, solitude and loneliness look the same, as both are about being alone. However, they are very different under the surface.

Loneliness feels negative, with a sense of isolation and that there is something missing. Older people are often assumed to be most lonely, especially when they fall ill, lose mobility or lose a partner and live alone. Interestingly, while this group does experience emotional loneliness, research suggests loneliness tends to be highest in young people (ages 16 to 25), including young people who appear to be well-connected and popular. It is possible to be with people and still feel lonely due to lack of meaningful connections. A 2015 survey funded by VicHealth found that one in eight young people reported a very high intensity of loneliness.

Solitude, on the other hand, is the state of being alone without feeling lonely. It is positive and desirable, as it provides space to enjoy your own company. Solitude is an opportunity for reflection, inner searching or growth or enjoyment of some kind, whether it be reading, time in nature, creative arts or meditation.

While I certainly do not claim that learning to appreciate solitude is going to solve the loneliness epidemic, valuing quiet time alone may alleviate the individual's pain by helping them to experience some positivity from being alone.

Poor thinking

Have you noticed how your thinking becomes clouded when you are overwhelmed? Have you noticed that you are on autopilot and not consciously thinking when you are busy doing and reacting? When we don't step back, slow down and think properly, we make assumptions and biased choices.

Nobel Prize–winning behavioural economist Daniel Kahneman highlights the prevalence and associated dangers of fast thinking (System 1 thinking) in his book *Thinking, Fast and Slow*. System 1 thinking – the fast, intuitive, autopilot thinking – is useful in simple everyday situations. However, it can make rushed decisions based on biased, illogical thinking and misinformation.

One of the biggest problems with System 1 thinking is that it seeks to create a coherent and plausible explanation for what is happening by relying on associations and memories, pattern-matching and assumptions. We default to the story even if that story is based on incorrect information.

Raymond Kethledge and Michael S. Erwin, authors of *Lead Yourself First: Inspiring leadership through solitude* share numerous examples of leaders who deliberately use solitude to ensure their leadership effectiveness. One of the reasons these leaders use solitude is to develop clarity of thinking, which aids in building convictions and courage not to conform with the norm or what is expected. Clarity, conviction and courage are *not* accessed by keeping busy or being distracted.

Recent studies are showing that taking time for silence restores the nervous system, helps sustain energy, and conditions our minds to be more adaptive and responsive to the complex environments in which so many of us now live, work and lead. Duke Medical School's Imke Kirste recently found that silence is associated with the development of new cells in the hippocampus, the key brain region associated with learning and memory.

Gianpiero Petriglieri, an Associate Professor of Organisational Behaviour at INSEAD, advocates for active self-reflection as a component to becoming a better leader. He claims that all the leadership courses taught at all the finest business schools in the world are completely worthless without it. This is because a leader's inability to improve is based on an inability to change and an inability, or unwillingness, to reflect on his or her experiences in order to bring about change.

Self-reflection is hard work. It requires you to challenge your own thinking and assumptions, and sometimes these are deeply held beliefs about what has made you successful so far. Without the quiet space to do this self-reflection, however, no amount of training will make a difference. Coaching will facilitate self-reflection and will challenge our thinking, but ultimately, we need to create the quiet space, do the hard work and make the conscious choice to apply the new thinking.

Lost creativity

The undervaluing of both our quiet nature and our time is also undermining our ability to be creative, not just for those who are naturally quiet, but for everyone. Research shows that individual reflection and thinking is the source of intuitive, creative ideas, as this quiet space allows for the mind to wander and for ideas to connect, evolve and generate insights.

In their book *Lead Yourself First*, Raymond Kethledge and Michael S. Erwin identified that creativity requires solitude and reflection:

> *As with clarity, there is an intuitive path to creativity, on which much of the work is already done for the leader, if only he will pause to listen… Intuition can make connections not only between certain facts that usually come bundled together, but also between things that at first seem unrelated or even antagonistic.*

They refer to Sir Isaac Newton, who intuited the law of gravity – the basis of astrophysics and the movement of planets in their orbits – based on a falling apple. He is an example of quiet self-reflection: he connected disparate ideas while sitting quietly under a tree.

Dr Jason Fox also encourages organisational leaders to question default thinking. In working with leadership teams, he calls out the default thinking and questions whether it is helping or hindering the organisation's future success. He said:

> *Default thinking saves us time and makes us more efficient. We need it for about 80 per cent of the work we do. But my worry is that for many organisations, 98 per cent of the time is spent thinking by default… and this just increases the chance that you'll move closer to future irrelevance. It's important to make distinctions between meaningful progress and that which could be considered a 'delusion of progress' (productivity without value).*

Information overload, distractions and noise only allow for reactive thinking and reinforcement of the status quo. Without quiet space and time to challenge default thinking, people are only capable of doing what's worked before. Original ideas do not generate out of default thinking and replicating others' ideas.

Poor communication

One of the many frustrating conversations I've had involved a senior manager who was very articulate and skilled at asking perceptive questions. Whenever we had meetings, however, it felt like he was directing the conversation to suit him. At times it felt like an interrogation, rather than a connected and meaningful conversation.

I had a meeting with him just before I left his team. It was an opportunity to share my experiences and hear his feedback on what I could do moving forward. He began the meeting by thanking me for my contributions and congratulating me on the move: a good start. He then moved onto giving me feedback and the lessons I could take into my next role. He asked me for my reflections on the feedback, but long before I could finish sharing my reflections, he moved onto the next question. I started to answer his question, but again, before I could finish, he asked me about my career aspirations. At the time, it felt to me like he wanted a quick answer and a quick meeting, just to show that he was doing the right thing. He fired question after question, often not related to my answers. Time was up and it didn't feel like we'd had a meaningful conversation at all.

Poor communication often stems from undervaluing our quieter skills.

Poor listening

Most communication training focuses on speaking. At best, listening might get a module or so and people generally learn techniques for active listening. Yet without listening, how can there be communication?

Whether it's the obvious, distracted listening, the more covert, pretending to listen or the listening to respond, poor listening is not only a killer of communication, but it is a killer of trust. So many people say, 'If only they would listen' when talking about relationships that are not working well, whether in the workplace or at home.

Oscar Trimboli, author of *Deep Listening: How to make an impact beyond words*, says that:

> *We spend 55 per cent of our time listening during the day, yet 2 per cent of the world has been trained on how to listen. For individuals, leaders, teams and organisations the most impactful communication isn't about how eloquently and persuasively you speak, but how consciously, deliberately and skilfully you listen to your employees, customers and markets.*

Poor listening results in unproductive meetings, random activities, siloed organisations, damaged trust with staff, customers and stakeholders, disengaged staff and so on. Listening should be front and centre of communication.

Not being influenced by what you hear

Not only do we not listen well, we do not properly consider and are not influenced by what has been said. 'Yes, but…' is the common sign that indicates unwillingness to be influenced. Our minds are too full of our own ideas and justifications about why we are right. There is no quiet reflection or space for other's ideas to mingle with our own.

Roger Schwartz, author of *Smart Leaders, Smarter Teams*, observed over 30 years that many leaders get stuck in the mindset of unilateral control, where they try to achieve goals by influencing others without being influenced in return. A unilateral control mindset creates poor decisions, resistance to change, defensiveness and stress.

Without being influenced by what we hear, our communication is a monologue pretending to be a dialogue.

No silence

Many people are uncomfortable with silence in conversations. Without silence, however, there is no space to think or absorb what has been said. Without silence, the words simply float over our heads and do not sink in. Speech becomes noise rather than information.

The best speakers use pauses deliberately to create impact, and to ensure key messages land with the audience. The best coaches use silence to allow people to reflect and do the hard thinking required for transformational insights to emerge. Susan Scott, author of *Fierce Conversations*, said, 'Let silence do the heavy lifting' when you are having high stakes and difficult conversations. The best negotiators don't jump in to fill the silence, they use silence to be deliberate about what and how much they share and to think about what has already been said. The best salespeople use silence to allow people time to make a decision.

Rushed speaking is also related to the lack of silence in conversations. What is it like to try and understand people who speak fast, who rattle out words without taking a breath? They either speak fast naturally or their anxiety causes them to rush their speech. Rushed speaking confuses people and reduces impact.

Richard Lawton, Master Voice Coach and author of *Raise Your Voice*, teaches people to slow down and speak more clearly by asking people to deliberately focus on the end consonant of each word. He also encourages people to breathe and use pauses.

Being comfortable with silence during interactions will improve communication in many ways.

Lack of space and safety

When leaders provide limited space for people to speak, don't ask helpful questions to draw out relevant information, or are not consciously creating psychological safety, communication becomes one way. The leader will say what they need to say, and the team will either say very little or say what the leader wants to hear.

I have worked with many leaders who complain that people don't speak up or ask questions. What happens quite often is that the leader may ask, 'What are your thoughts?' or 'Do you have any questions?' and move on after half a second of silence. Someone might say something that the leader disagrees with and the leader will overtly or subtly shut down the comment without acknowledging the contribution. As soon as that happens, the safety to speak up disappears for the whole group. The inability to create space and genuinely listen is one of the most overlooked communication errors.

So much communication effort is focused on speaking and writing – the transmitting side of communication – while the receiving side and the container for effective communication receive insufficient attention.

~

Human minds *need* quiet – some more than others, but we *all* need it, not just introverts.

If our quiet nature has such potential value, you may be asking, why don't quiet professionals just step up?

Unfortunately, if it was as easy as telling them to step up, we wouldn't have the issue of wasted talent that we currently have. The reasons for many talented people remaining quiet and hidden are complex. Part II will explore this.

Part II

Talent in hiding

WHEN WE TALK about quiet people, most assume we are talking about introverts. Having met, spoken with or heard from thousands of people from around the world who are interested in the Quietly Powerful movement, though, this is not always the case.

While many books and articles have been written about introverts, I have encountered many ambiverts (people with both introvert and extrovert preferences) and even extroverts who face the challenge of being quietly disempowered in the professional context.

Part II will explore the reasons why people remain quietly disempowered beyond introversion. These reasons include what we are born with, our upbringing, and the environment and narrative around being quiet.

Chapter 4

Personality

Introversion

I was on a tour of a new office of an organisation with state-of-the-art technology and design. The senior leader who was hosting the tour proudly showed us the various rooms, open areas and sections of the large office space. We saw interactive whiteboards in an open space for informal collaboration, video conferencing and collaboration tools, team task-tracking tools and more. A lot of the layout was based on an open plan office design with the intention of boosting communication and cross-functional collaboration, as most supporters of open plan office design tend to advocate.

    We moved into an area where there were groups of desks with a few people sitting and working quietly. They seemed absorbed in what they were working on. The hosting senior leader looked at those people, smiled, and said, 'A lot of our team are introverts; they need help to talk to each other and collaborate'. I looked at my colleague with raised eyebrows and felt sympathy for the people at the desks who may have heard the comment.

Introversion is becoming more widely accepted thanks to authors and speakers like Susan Cain, author of *Quiet: The power of introverts in a world that can't stop talking*, Laurie Helgoe, author of *Introvert Power*, Matthew Pollard, author of *The Introvert's Edge*, Jennifer Kahnweiler, author of *The Introvert Leader* and many more.

Even with greater acknowledgement of the value of introversion, stereotypes remain strong and introversion can still be perceived as inferior to extroversion. Unfortunately, psychologists in the past have written about introversion as a disorder. For decades 'introverted personality' and 'introverted disorder of childhood' have been in the World Health Organization's manual, the International Statistical Classification of Diseases and Related Health Problems (ICD-9 CM). Scarily, the American Psychiatric Association's forthcoming Diagnostic and Statistical Manual (DSM-5) was going to include introversion as a contributing factor in diagnosing personality disorders as recently as 2011. Fortunately, it was removed by 2012.

Even though we have (hopefully) passed the era where we saw introversion as a disorder, we still hear subtle comments about introversion as being inferior or needing help, such as the comment by the senior leader about his introvert team. We never hear comments like, 'They are extroverts, they need help to listen to each other'.

Other times, introverts are discriminated against. An HR professional told me that the parent company of his firm had used a personality profiling tool as part of their talent assessment process and eliminated candidates who showed up as introverts. The assumption was that introverts did not have leadership potential. Just like sexism and racism, 'personality-ism' exists.

Matthew Kuofie, Dana Stephens-Craig and Richard Dool wrote in their paper, 'An Overview Perception of Introverted Leaders', 'Just like any stereotype that has held humans back from their full potential (i.e. racism, sexism, ageism, homosexuality, religious beliefs, etc.) the label of introversion in business carries that same type of oppressive nature.'

In addition, introversion is misunderstood.

As it is popularly used, the term 'extroverted' is understood to mean sociable or outgoing, while the term 'introverted' is understood to mean shy or withdrawn. Carl Jung, however, originally intended the words to have an entirely different meaning. He used them to describe the preferred focus of one's energy: on either the outer or the inner world. Extroverts orient their energy to the outer world, while introverts orient their energy to the inner world.

Paul Boasman described his introversion very much as a preference for the inner world. He said:

I'm someone who gets energy from inside myself and I know I could exist happily on a desert island for months on end on my own. I also find big groups tiring. It's almost like too much energy. It wears me down, so I have to step back from it and refresh and reflect. The best work I have done has often involved times when I have been able to step back, sit on my own and think about things.

Yamini Naidu, who has been a professional speaker for more than ten years, said that a lot of her fellow professional speakers are introverts. She said:

The way we recharge and re-energise offstage is often alone. If you're a speaker and you're spending a lot of your time on planes and in airports, lounges and hotel rooms, you actually are alone. You have to learn to really love and enjoy your own company... I relish it because it's such a contrast to the very public face my role has.

Despite the efforts of introverts trying to explain otherwise, they are regularly stereotyped as being shy, anti-social, not confident, analytical, having a detailed focus and being organised and structured, not good with people or groups of people, not good at networking, uncharismatic, not very talkative, softly spoken or bookworms.

Firstly, not all introverts have all these qualities. I know a few confident, gregarious, totally chaotic and disorganised introverts! They may show these qualities differently or they may be using learned behaviours. As mentioned, introversion is primarily about getting energy from the inside. Other qualities, preferences, behaviours and skills can vary from introvert to introvert.

Secondly, most personality assessment tools – certainly those based on the Big Five personality traits that many psychological researchers use – show that we are a combination of sub-elements within the introvert–extrovert scale. For example, a person may be sociable but not so gregarious and excitement-seeking. They are more likely to spend a lot of time with friends they know but are not as comfortable going out to meet new people or going on new adventures. Their friends may see them as an extrovert, but personality tools may show them as more of an introvert, as a combined result of the sub-elements. We are on a spectrum of introversion and extroversion and usually not completely one or the other.

We have a mix of qualities and how we express them can depend on the situation and environment. I know many introverts who are chatty when they are talking about their favourite topic but become quiet when the conversation shifts to an unfamiliar area. In addition, we are a blend of many other personality traits, which I will go into shortly.

Thirdly, we are all able to develop skills and learned behaviours. Some of the best performers (actors, comedians, presenters, etc.) have introvert preferences. Emma Watson, Audrey Hepburn, Lady Gaga, Robin Williams, Bill Gates, Elton John and Warren Buffett are just a few of the many well-known, highly talented and successful introverts. With purpose, intent and practice, introverts can combine our natural talents and learned skills and behaviours to succeed in many fields.

Liz Compton, an experienced senior HR executive who is now Director, People & Culture at Auto & General, sees her introversion as a preference, as different situations require different leadership styles. She suggests that we regularly ask ourselves, 'What type of leadership is useful right now?' so that we deliberately amplify our preferred style or adjust to another style.

Cambridge personality researcher Dr Brian Little shares in his book, *Me, Myself and Us: The science of personality and the art of well-being*, that we all have what's called 'Free Traits' where we can act out of our usual character for the purpose of a passion project or a cause that matters to us. The energetic performer, passionate speaker and flamboyant entertainer are examples of people using their Free Trait for a purpose.

For all the above reasons, deciding whether a person is an introvert or extrovert, and what kind of person he or she is by simply seeing one aspect of that person, is not very helpful.

People labelled as introverts are often seen as quiet and hidden because of these stereotypes and misunderstandings. Unfortunately, those of us with introvert tendencies may also feel inadequate and misunderstood because of the way people talk about introverts and box them in.

If you are more introverted, do you appreciate your introverted nature? If you are not, what assumptions do you make about your introverted colleagues, friends and family members?

Introversion is not the only reason why someone may have a quieter nature. Other Big Five personality traits can cause someone to be quieter than others. We'll look at three of these – agreeableness, high emotionality and high sensitivity – over the rest of this chapter.

Agreeableness

A coaching client of mine, let's call her Leila, was a highly competent IT professional with a track record of delivering projects. She was well-regarded by her colleagues, and a previous manager tapped her on the shoulder to join an IT consulting firm where he worked. She accepted his offer, as she appreciated being valued as a team member and she knew she could do the job well.

The first few months went well, but after the 'honeymoon' period, she started to experience some tension with the sales team. They kept pushing back on the pricing estimates that Leila was putting forward, and sometimes going ahead with their prices rather than Leila's estimates. This under-pricing by the sales team caused problems down the track when delivering projects, as the project teams ran out of budget to do the quality job they promised to deliver.

Leila was high on agreeableness and disliked disagreements. She would feel anxious as the tension built and would struggle to find words to explain her side of the story. Whenever there was a disagreement with the sales team, she was unable to properly explain her rationale because of her anxiety about upsetting them. She also felt that she did not have the experience or authority to be direct.

Leila's inability to stand her ground was beginning to impact more of the projects under delivery. Even though she had the knowledge, expertise and experience, she was unable to do the job as well as she hoped. Through our coaching sessions, I challenged her beliefs about being direct and its impact. She was overestimating the negative impact and underestimating the value of transparency. We practiced some ways she could be clearer and more direct without it feeling like confrontation to her. She started small and gradually grew more comfortable.

Agreeable individuals find it important to get along with others and they are often willing to put aside their interests for other people. These individuals are helpful, friendly, considerate and generous. Agreeableness is an advantage for building teams and maintaining harmony, but can cause people to hold back from speaking up to avoid potential conflict.

A number of other people I coach are more on the extrovert end, but are also considered quiet because they are naturally accommodating. Their profiles show that they are high on agreeableness and dislike conflict. People who are high on agreeableness, regardless of other personality traits, may hold back to avoid any kind of conversation that can feel like conflict. For them, what others call debate can feel like conflict, too. Many stay quiet, hoping that the conversation will move on or the issue will go away, which can be unhelpful in the long run.

It is more natural and easier for agreeable individuals to go along with the group and remain hidden. Agreeable people are often seen as friendly, but also as 'soft', as they do not overtly disagree with others. Being quiet and soft is not seen as leader-worthy, which results in agreeable individuals being overlooked.

If you are high on agreeableness, how have you used it to address conflict rather than avoid it? If you know highly agreeable people, how have you made it safer for them to speak more directly?

High emotionality

Another coaching client, let's call her Shelly, was a successful senior executive. She was a perfectionist and always questioned whether she had done enough. The feedback she received from her supervisors, peers, team and clients was about her reliability, focus on quality and service.

The one difficulty that Shelly had was speaking in groups. Even if she knew the topic well, she would get nervous, her face would go red and she would stumble over her words. Having a group of people looking at her speak would freeze her brain; she would struggle to explain things that she knew well and being put on the spot with a question caused her to panic.

The worst was when she had to stand up and give presentations. She would get so anxious that she would start feeling sick a few days before the presentation. Shelly admitted in our coaching sessions that there had been times when she had avoided presenting in the past by saying that she was unwell.

Our coaching focused on a range of strategies to manage her anxiety, including dealing with her inner critic by finding ways to make public speaking feel like a normal conversation.

Shelly was ten out of ten on emotionality using the Facet5 personality assessment tool we used, meaning that she experienced her emotions more intensely than most. (In the Big Five personality traits, 'emotionality' is called 'neuroticism'.) The thought of giving a presentation hit her significantly harder than someone with a lower score, even if they were just as afraid of public speaking.

While Shelly was also an introvert, what drove her to remain hidden the most was her emotionality. She would avoid public speaking, being the centre of attention in groups and speaking up in group meetings. This meant that people did not know her capabilities unless they worked with her directly.

Interestingly, Shelly is not the only person I have coached with high emotionality. One third to a half of my coaching clients have high emotionality. Their natural tendency to feel intensely has resulted in a fear of speaking up, trying new things and stepping into leadership roles. When they recognise this and find ways to consciously manage their emotions and inner voices, they start making small steps towards managing their anxieties.

People who score high in emotionality are very emotionally sensitive. They have an emotional response to events that would not affect people with lower scores. This sensitivity can be beneficial in picking up others' moods and responding considerately. However, a high-scoring individual may find it difficult to think clearly and cope with stress, and they might doubt themselves more.

High emotionality isn't always shown on the outside, so some people with high emotionality are perceived to be calm and able to handle stress. However, when it comes to speaking up, many of them express their anxiety about what others may think of them and experience self-doubt about contributing anything valuable. As a result, speaking up and being put on the spot when they were not prepared became stressful.

Regardless of where we are on the introversion–extroversion scale, we can be high on emotionality. The only difference is how overtly the emotions are expressed. The more introverted and/or agreeable you are, the more likely you will suppress emotions. By trying to hide your stress, anxiety or frustration, however, you may present as being quiet and moody.

Remaining hidden may be a survival mechanism due to these anxieties, regardless of your introversion/extroversion preferences.

If you are high on emotionality, what strategies do you use to manage your anxieties? If you know people with high emotionality, how do you support them to use emotional sensitivity as a strength and to deal with the personal costs of emotionality?

Highly Sensitive People

I have a friend, who I will call Cara, who is highly energetic, enthusiastic, talkative and social. From what I know, she loves to go out with friends, is energised by group workshops, laughs loudly and is friendly to people she meets for the first time. She is clearly on the extrovert end of the spectrum. On the other hand, she lives on a farm and loves to go outside on her own, and she finds she needs to get away from her two young children to get some peace and quiet. I have also seen her become quiet and reflective in a group setting, which is not the usual Cara I know.

I found out that she is a highly sensitive extrovert.

In addition to the Big Five personality traits, people with Sensory Processing Sensitivity (SPS) can become quiet as well. A Highly Sensitive Person (HSP) is characterised by deep information processing, high emotional responsiveness and empathy and heightened awareness of environmental subtleties, and they are easily overstimulated. HSPs are not necessarily reacting emotionally, so it's different from emotionality. They are more aware of their surroundings and are more easily aroused, not necessarily fearful and anxious. According to research by Elaine Aron, author of *The Highly Sensitive Person*, about 20 per cent of the population are HSPs. Elaine writes:

> *Highly sensitive people are more conscientious. They notice certain details others may overlook, and they can be very creative. Being a highly sensitive person doesn't mean you have a disorder that needs to be fixed. It simply means that you process sensory data more deeply.*

HSPs can be deep in thought or may be overstimulated and overwhelmed such that they retreat. For HSPs, being quiet is an energy management strategy. As with people who have the other personality traits mentioned so far, they can be misunderstood. Cara told me that she was relieved when she realised she was an extrovert HSP, as she could explain this to people when she needed some quiet time.

Extrovert HSPs can swing from being very social and talkative to suddenly needing time out on their own, which can be confusing to others. Introvert HSPs will retreat even further than usual when overwhelmed, preferring solitude and quiet even more than non-HSPs who have an introvert preference.

If you are highly sensitive, what strategies do you have to avoid becoming overwhelmed while using your sensitivity as a strength? If you are not an HSP, how aware are you of those who are and how accommodating are you to their needs?

~

Of course, personality traits are not the only contributor to being quiet and hidden. Upbringing also has a great deal of influence, as we'll explore in the next chapter.

Chapter 5

Upbringing

Many people are challenged by their conditioning to not speak up against authority or against mainstream views. I know of extroverts who are very chatty and social with friends and family, but who clam up in the workplace. Many professionals from Asian cultures have shared this challenge with me, but there are many others who have similar kinds of conditioning.

Culture

During year 10 at my co-ed public high school in Japan, they separated the girls and boys one day to have a 'talk' about the roles of women and men and how we should behave. We girls got a lecture about how the primary role of women is to support men. While I don't remember exactly what was said, I distinctly remember the underlying message suggesting that women should be in the shadows. I remember thinking that that didn't sit well with me, but I noticed the other girls simply accepted it without questioning. Looking back, I wonder what the boys were told about their roles and how they should treat women. This was 1986.

Soon after, I escaped this Japanese school and went to Canada as an exchange student, then to Australia to finish school and go to university. It was my way of rebelling against Japanese cultural norms as a teenager. While I physically escaped, nonetheless I internalised some of the cultural norms, and it has taken me decades to address them. I notice that some of these cultural norms still hold me back. For example, my fear of standing out and being the centre of attention was partly due to my personality but also due to my cultural (and gendered) conditioning.

I acknowledge upfront that exploring being Asian is complex and that I cannot possibly cover the complexities in one chapter. The various countries in Asia are different in some ways and similar in others. There are also differences between first- and second-generation Asians in a Western culture, like myself: I was born in Australia and have spent more of my life in Australia.

What I can highlight, however, are the common challenges Asians face around being quiet or hidden. Many people of Asian heritage have attended the Quietly Powerful talks and have agreed with what I spoke about, so I am certain that these commonalities exist:

- **Fitting in.** In many East Asian cultures, the social pressure to conform is enormous. Being hierarchical and collectivistic (as opposed to individualistic), these cultures value conformity above individuality. People are pressured to do all that they can to maintain the status quo and an appearance of harmony, even if it's at the expense of individual autonomy, voice or needs. There is an invisible and assumed judgement about being different.

- **Not challenging authority.** From a young age, many Asian children are taught not to challenge authority – parents, elders, teachers, authority figures in uniform and so on – and get into trouble when they do. Rules set by authority are to be obeyed. Of course, some rebel, but there is pressure from above and from peers to conform. Questioning authority is a sign of disrespect and individual expression is not encouraged. A little voice in the head constantly censors what you say and tells you off: 'You can't say that!'

- **Saving face.** Closely related is the notion of saving face. If you suspect that someone will be embarrassed by you saying something, it is not to be shared. This belief is particularly strong in relation to authority figures, but it can also apply to peers. Again, the inner censor is closely managing whether you say something, what you say and how you say it.
- **Not talking yourself (or your family) up.** It's common for many people to feel awkward about talking themselves up. The tall poppy syndrome is very strong in many Asians, and many Eastern religious teachings and traditions value humility. I notice in myself sometimes that I feel proud of my daughter but feel hesitant about sharing her achievements with others. I downplay it and say she's still got more to improve on, even though I'm as proud as punch on the inside.

Stereotype challenges

Stereotypes about Asians are strong in Western societies. While some differences between Asian countries are acknowledged, stereotypes about being meek and reserved, hard-working and good at maths and science, for example, seem to stick, even though many Asians do not fit these stereotypes. The problem with stereotypes is that people make up their minds as soon as they see an Asian face, and their biased view colours every interaction and decision. We unconsciously select what we notice, which is what's called 'confirmation bias' – we look for and only see what we believe. For example, we only see an Asian person's unassertive side; when they are assertive, we miss it or see it as an exception. In turn, this perception impacts decisions in relation to promotion and performance reviews.

Asian women are particularly challenged by stereotypes of them as compliant, adaptable and gentle. They are expected to be dutiful daughters and charming wives, but not to be assertive or ambitious in their careers. It is difficult to go against these stereotypes. Their non-conforming attitudes or behaviours attract judgement from the Asian family and community, and they are not taken seriously by others.

Beyond being Asian, various other aspects of culture have an impact on our self-concept and how we should behave. Professor Geert Hofstede developed a framework for cross-cultural communication using factor analysis, based on a worldwide survey of employee values by IBM between 1967 and 1973. Further research has helped to refine his original framework and it continues to be a major resource in the field of cross-cultural psychology, describing national cultures along several characteristics. For example, it describes collectivist cultures as preferring a tightly knit framework in society in which individuals can expect their relatives or members of a particular ingroup to look after them in exchange for unquestioning loyalty. Individualist cultures, on the other hand, are described as preferring a loosely knit social framework in which individuals are expected to take care of only themselves and their immediate families.

You can see the contrast in news reports of how the black hole was first identified and photographed in individualist versus collectivist cultures. This is an incredible discovery and achievement in 2019, so I am by no means discrediting anyone on the team. What was interesting was how it was reported.

CNN attempted to give Dr Katie Bouman full credit, even though fellow researchers explained that she was only 'a major part of one of the imaging subteams'. BBC News was also eager to have a woman at the helm, and titled its article 'Katie Bouman: The woman behind the first black hole image'. Phys.org went even further, calling the young scientist a 'superstar' in its headline. This is even after Bouman herself made it clear on Facebook that she did not want sole credit for the achievement.

While the Western media attempted to celebrate the 'superstar', Asian publications, including *Asahi*, offered a more nuanced and truthful article, writing that '207 scientists in 17 nations and regions took part in the project', and refusing to assign the achievement to any one of the scientists.

Asian cultures are generally collectivist, but there are other countries that are also understood to be more collectivist than individualistic – according to Professor Geert Hofstede and his organisation's research. These include Egypt, Brazil, Ethiopia, Portugal, Romania and Russia.

People in collectivist cultures expect loyalty and can have a strong fear of rejection. When others' opinions of you matter more, you will watch what you say and may hold back to avoid rejection. So, if you were brought up in a collectivist culture, or even a family culture, you may have a deep fear of saying anything that would 'rock the boat' or cause anyone to lose face. You may also be averse to self-promotion, as it may be seen as bragging and being self-absorbed. The need to fit in, or the dread of standing out, may be a key factor to you being quiet or hidden.

Another characteristic that Professor Geert Hofstede and his organisation refer to is the Power Distance Index (PDI), which is the degree to which the less powerful members of a society accept and expect that power is distributed unequally. Societies with a large degree of Power Distance accept a hierarchical order in which everybody has a place, and which needs no further justification. In other words, a hierarchical culture. In societies with low Power Distance, people strive to equalise the distribution of power and demand justification for inequalities of power.

China, India, Russia and Romania are examples of countries with high PDI. You may also see differences in PDI in organisational or even family cultures.

Military organisations need to maintain a high PDI culture to ensure coordinated action, especially during times of operation in the field. As Simon Harrington, ex-Rear Admiral of the Royal Australian Navy said, '…if you're commanding a ship, you can only have one person manoeuvring the ship at any time. If you have two people giving different orders, confusion reigns'.

'Tiger parenting', often seen in Chinese families, involves expecting obedience and excellence in every endeavour. There is a high PDI culture in these families, where children are expected not to talk back and to do as they are told. Imagine trying to teach tiger parenting to a family growing up in a low PDI culture, such as the Netherlands, the United Kingdom or the United States. I envisage that it would feel foreign to the parents and the children would not have a bar of it!

When you are brought up in a cuture that is both collectivist and has a high PDI, speaking up against authority and standing out can be particularly difficult.

Can you see how your cultural background may play a part in whether you remain hidden or not? How have you reconciled your cultural conditioning against what you feel you need to do in your career? How sensitive are you to others' cultural conditioning and the impact it has on them?

Gender

My year 10 story of being told that a woman's role is to support men may sound extreme and old-fashioned. However, similar messages are still being received by girls at school and women in society, although in subtler ways.

Whether it's the type of toys girls and boys are given, the types of activities they are encouraged to take up or the extent to which they are noticed and recognised for speaking up or taking the lead, the consistent patterns in most countries around the world are that men are supposed to be strong, competitive and outspoken and women are supposed to be gentle, supportive and stay in the background.

In a fascinating BBC documentary called *No More Boys and Girls: Can our kids go gender free?*, Dr Javid Abdelmoneim experimented with removing all differences in the way boys and girls were treated in a year 3 classroom. Before the experiment, the children were interviewed about the differences between men and women. Boys said things like, 'Men are better because they are stronger, and they've got more jobs', and girls said things like, 'I think men are better at being in charge'. A series of research tests were conducted over a week and it showed that girls consistently underestimated how clever they were. The teacher confirmed some of the findings that the girls were quieter and appeared less confident in class.

This was despite neuroimaging showing that boys and girls brains were structurally indistinguishable. Modern neuroscience explains that the brain is very plastic (able to change) such that brain development is very entangled with society and the environment we live in. Abdelmoneim's hypothesis was that children's thoughts about themselves can be changed by how they are treated.

What was most interesting was how surprised the well-meaning teacher was about how differently he had been treating the boys and girls. For example, he was asking questions to boys (often the noisier ones) more often than to girls. He also called the girls 'love', 'sweet-pea' and 'darling' and called the boys 'mate', 'fella' and 'lad'. It was so ingrained that he simply didn't realise he had been doing so. It took some help from the students, as well as Abdelmoneim, for the teacher to change the way he behaved.

There are plenty of studies into gender dynamics, unconscious bias and stereotyping. Women tend to stay quieter and hidden and often do not compete for leadership positions. It is not due to their lack of abilities or potential, but due to ingrained and stereotypical ways in which they were treated as girls and how that continues into how they are treated as women in the workplace.

It is no wonder progress in gender diversity in senior leadership has been slow.

In her book *Stop Fixing Women*, Catherine Fox advocates for fixing the system that prevents women from progressing into leadership positions, rather than trying to fix the women. Women are regularly told to 'back themselves' and 'lean in', and are sent to women's leadership programs and conferences, as if they are solely responsible for breaking through the glass ceiling. A key message of her book is that, 'Telling women to change to fix the gender gap is more like victim blaming rather than empowerment'. If the system changes and women are treated differently to how they are now, they will be noticed, will be taken seriously and will take on leadership roles that they are capable of.

Dr Tomas Chamorro-Premuzic, in his book *Why Do So Many Incompetent Men Become Leaders? (And how to fix it)*, argues that 'the underrepresentation of women in leadership was not due to their lack of ability or motivation, but to our inability to detect incompetence in men'. His key message is to elevate the standards of leadership by reassessing the selection criteria and methods, rather than sending women to programs to help women emulate men. Too many overconfident, self-absorbed men (and women) are seen as charismatic and having leadership potential, while too many competent women and men are overlooked. The result, states Chamorro-Premuzic, 'in both business and politics is a surplus of incompetent men in charge, and this surplus reduces opportunities for competent people – women and men – while keeping the standards of leadership depressingly low'.

How aware are you of the impact on you of gendered conditioning and stereotypes? What strategies have you used to address them? How have you dealt with your own biases around who you consider to be leader-like?

Religious upbringing

In one of the public breakfasts, as I was sharing the challenges of being Asian and how conditioned I was to stay quiet and conform, one person in the room piped up and said that it is not just about being Asian. She shared how her strict Catholic upbringing had shaped her fear of speaking against authority – that she would never disagree or argue with her parents, teachers or priests. She was taught to be a 'good girl': to be compliant. As a group, we reflected on how else we may have been conditioned and realised that there are many combinations and permutations that cause us to behave the way we do.

One of my friends and colleagues, Jo, who is quite a chatty extrovert, shared a story of her school years in a Catholic girls' school. Girls who were doing well in academics and sports were not recognised, and outspoken girls were not well thought of. She sensed that competitiveness and standing out was viewed negatively by the nuns, and there was a sense of guilt and shame associated with it.

Jo had a best friend in year 4 who was an all-round high achiever, both in academics and sports. Jo was very good at sports too, like her friend, but was often just behind her in academics. You would think that having such a good example for a friend would be a good thing.

Jo's parents, however, were told by a nun at their parent–teacher interview that her friend was a 'bad influence' on her and that they should not spend so much time together. While she cannot remember exactly how, Jo was affected by this comment and the friends drifted apart over their primary school years.

Jo internalised some of these messages and has had to work on overcoming these voices which have stopped her from achieving the best in her work. While she is not a quiet person socially, she found herself holding back or not speaking up when there was a risk of standing out or being seen as too assertive.

Even if it's not a cultural conditioning, you may have had an upbringing in which you were expected to fear and comply with authority, or to not stand out or brag. Most traditional school systems rewarded compliance and punished disobedience. Often, girls are expected to and are praised for being 'good'. This leads to a belief that it is safer to fit in, even if we have to pretend.

Are you aware of any religious messages that have been internalised which have not been helpful? How have you countered the unhelpful messages while listening to the helpful ones?

School and family

A coaching client, who I will call Sharon, was troubled by her difficulty in speaking confidently with senior management. Sharon was well regarded: her team described her as a collaborative, empowering leader who supported the team to perform at their best. Her peers described her as someone who influenced their thinking and was a solid contributor of ideas. Yet in her 360-degree feedback report, she received comments about improving her communication and influencing skills. Sharon wasn't surprised, as she knew that she had trouble being clear and concise when communicating with senior leaders.

While she acknowledged that it happened to others as well, Sharon reflected further about the reasons for her anxiety and withdrawal in the company of senior people. She noticed her inner voice seemed to put senior people on a pedestal; it would assume they were more knowledgeable than her or they would think of her ideas and issues as insignificant or think that she was not worthy of being in their presence.

When she heard the inner voice of 'not worthy', Sharon recalled her childhood experiences of being brought up in a poor family in the country. She clearly remembered both her mother and grandmother telling her not to visit her friends who were better off than them – that they wouldn't appreciate having her over. She would never have friends over, either, as her mother was embarrassed about their destitute house. She had internalised these messages of feeling inferior in the presence of those who appeared to be better off or a higher rank than her.

There are invisible and internal reasons for putting ourselves down and remaining in hiding. There could be other childhood experiences which may have disempowered people. It could be that they were bullied at school, subjected to racism, homophobia or another form of discrimination, or told that they wouldn't amount to much by teachers or parents. It could be that they were neglected due to being in a troubled family, whether it was related to alcoholism, drugs or family violence. Whatever those experiences, we internalise them as a reflection of our own worth, often without realising.

We may not even realise these life experiences are affecting how we behave in the workplace. While some of these realisations may be difficult to face, doing so gives you the opportunity to address them rather than being driven by them.

Are you aware of messages you heard in your childhood that hold you back? Are they strong voices in your mind? How have you dealt with them so they don't affect you as much?

~

All of the above-mentioned authors, researchers and stories highlight the significant effect of environment and conditioning on how people are seen and recognised or remain hidden in the workplace. Being quiet and hidden is not just due to what the individual is born with, it's also a result of the environment in which they were brought up and the environment in which they exist now.

Chapter 6

Power dynamics: Minority and rank

Power dynamics also contribute to people remaining quiet and hidden. When people feel less powerful, for whatever reason, they are more cautious in speaking up and can be silenced. While we often associate power dynamics with hierarchy and positional rank, other factors add to the complex forces of power and rank. Julie Diamond, author of *Power: A user's guide*, defines power as 'our capacity to impact and influence our environment' and states that power can be 'bestowed by virtue of our social status or position' or can be 'personal power that is grown and developed'.

A feeling of not belonging to the mainstream can reduce our sense of power. It could arise because you are in the minority with regards to gender, ethnicity, religion, sexual orientation, physical abilities, physical appearance, personality or thinking style, because you hold an unpopular opinion or are new to the group, or simply because you don't feel included. You may also feel powerless because of poor use of power by those with high rank, whether deliberate or unintended. When we feel we have less power, it takes courage, energy and personal power to speak up.

The silencing effect of power differences

You may have heard the term, 'career limiting move' (CLM). Most of the CLMs that I hear about have involved speaking up to those in power. The assumption is that when you speak against, give feedback to or disagree with those above you in the hierarchy, your career may be limited because they will no longer support you, or worse, will actively sabotage your career.

You hear well-meaning senior leaders telling employees to be open and honest and assuring them that there will be no repercussions for what they say. But how often do you see people being completely honest and direct? Some leaders have never been given direct feedback about poor behaviour because everyone is afraid of speaking to them. Anonymous feedback is the only way to obtain real feedback in most places. In some places, however, even anonymous feedback is not honest, because people fear that they could be traced.

Some organisations have a 'good news culture' in which bad news cannot go up the chain, as the consequences for the individuals raising issues are not worth the effort. The Royal Commission into Misconduct in the Banking, Superannuation and Financial Services Industry identified plenty of examples in which unethical, sometimes illegal, or costly actions and mistakes were made and not reported.

I know of many individuals, some of them normally confident and articulate, who become anxious and unable to speak up when senior leaders are present. This could partly be due to their upbringing and personality, as already discussed, but the environment created by those in power has a lot to do with it as well. These are examples of the silencing effect of hierarchical power dynamics.

What about all the people who have been sexually, physically or psychologically abused or harassed at work, home or elsewhere, and have been too afraid to speak up? Those who are not involved, especially those are in positions of power, might ask, 'Why didn't you speak up earlier?' Often, the victims don't feel safe enough to speak to or against those in power.

As Dr Stephen Schuitevoerder, international facilitator and teacher in process-oriented psychology, says, 'People with power and high rank are unconscious of the impact that they have on those with less power and rank'. None of us is immune. Let's say we welcome new people into a well-established, tight-knit team. We may like to think that we are equal and that we can talk freely. In reality, however, the new people are usually hesitant, and the ones with a higher rank – the old team members – need to make the effort to connect with them personally to help them feel more comfortable.

Power dynamics in organisations are felt but generally not discussed. You may find that the following groups have higher rank in many contexts:

- P&L (revenue-generating) divisions over support units
- those who do strategy work over those who perform front-line or operational work
- people who are working on the CEO's top priority projects over business-as-usual (BAU) work
- people from head office over those from other offices
- men over women
- Caucasian people over those of other ethnicities
- people in their thirties and forties over those younger or older
- extroverts over introverts
- people without disabilities over those with disabilities

- heterosexual over LGBTIQ+ people
- people who are analytical over those who are emotional.

In general, being in the mainstream in-group gives a feeling of relative high power compared to being in the out-group. Those in the mainstream can unintentionally marginalise people who are not, and this can have a silencing effect on those who feel that they less have power and are on the outer.

Power and rank are not only multi-faceted but also dynamic, in that the power differential depends on the context and who is involved. For example, a highly technical, experienced technology executive may feel powerful while sitting on an experts' panel at a technology conference, but less powerful in a business strategy meeting with the CEO.

Creating an environment in which it's safe to speak up and challenge authority requires a conscious effort on the part of leaders, and it rarely happens. So many leaders expect people in their teams and organisations to speak up without first addressing the power imbalances, and thereby create an unsafe environment. Of course, some people develop the courage, skills and personal power to speak out regardless, but others remain quiet, as the risks are too high.

How often have you taken the safe path and remained quiet? If you are a leader, how aware are you of these power dynamics and your impact as a leader?

When speaking up is unsafe

Lisa Evans, Director of Speaking Savvy, had a period in her career during which she experienced workplace bullying. She was in a toxic environment and became the target of bullying because she spoke up about some unacceptable behaviours towards others. She was shocked, because she had never experienced bullying at school or in her career until then. She lost her self-confidence and stopped speaking up, and it impacted her career: she saw others being noticed and getting the opportunities and promotions, even if they were not the smartest, most skilled or experienced people. They were the ones who were constantly putting up their hand and speaking up. She spoke of her experience:

> *I felt as though, if I was brave enough to speak up in a meeting, I would be interrupted, somebody would talk over the top of me, or they would then claim my idea as their own – all those sorts of things that I'm sure a lot of introverts have experienced. But this all became that much more intense when I was experiencing this bullying.*

Sadly, Lisa is not alone in experiencing bullying in the workplace. Safe Work Australia's 'National Data Set for Bullying and Harassment in Australian Workplaces' paints a grim picture:

- One in three women who lodged a WorkCover claim for a mental disorder stated it involved harassment or bullying.
- One in five men who made a WorkCover claim for a mental disorder stated it involved harassment or bullying.
- Some 37 per cent of workers reported being sworn at or yelled at in the workplace.

When you consider that these are only the reported cases, you can imagine how unsafe some organisations would feel for people. Speaking up would be the last thing on their minds.

This is an example of misuse of power that is not only disempowering, but toxic.

Being part of a minority or an outsider

Most professional women can think of times when they or their female colleagues have been ignored, interrupted or not taken seriously, or when others (often male colleagues) are credited for their ideas. Sadly, even my daughter has experienced this at

Power dynamics: Minority and rank

school, when she was ten years old. She was in a group of boys and girls deciding on a strategy for a game of passing the ball around as quickly as possible. The group was discussing a particular strategy that she thought wouldn't work, and she tried to explain why. The group ignored the idea, until a boy spoke up and said the same thing!

The issue of not being heard when you speak is exacerbated when you are the only woman in the room. It can feel as if you are invisible.

Susan Middleditch was a senior executive in the (male-dominated) construction industry, and recalled times when she had to be more forthright and assertive:

> *I was actually the first senior female executive in an organisation about 10 years ago and that was in the construction industry, so they [the men] have a particular nature about them. I had to be more upfront and forthright and a bit more bullish until they got used to me. I had to start like that because if I didn't, I'd never get a word in at the table.*

As a naturally quieter person, it took her a lot of energy, effort and courage to be more forthright than she normally was. She had to remind herself of the unique contribution she brought to the group:

> *I remember a couple of times where I said to them, 'Look, you have obviously recruited me into this role because you want and appreciate a different view, and so therefore, here's my different view'.*

She found that she was able to get back to her own quieter style once people understood the value she brought. Being in the minority, however, took a lot more energy.

As a person in the minority, how have you overcome the challenges of speaking up, being heard and taken seriously? If you are in the mainstream, how aware are you of those in the minority and the challenges they face?

Difficulty expressing contrary ideas

In 2018, SurveyMonkey partnered with Paradigm, a consulting firm that specialises in diversity and inclusion, to survey 843 working Americans. They found that 44 per cent of employees didn't feel that they could express a contrary opinion at work without fearing negative consequences.

In an organisation in which the leader has strong views, dominating or critical, it can be near impossible for anyone to speak up against their views. This also happens when there is an unwritten rule of not speaking against authority or a story about someone was persecuted for speaking up. What you then end up with is a team or organisation full of 'yes people'. 'Yes people' regularly fall into groupthink and do not challenge the status quo. These people go quiet or say what they think the boss wants to hear when they are asked a question or are invited to contribute ideas.

An inability for leaders to draw out contrary views is costly for an organisation. One organisation I worked with had a major IT failure during an upgrade that affected customers and caused it significant reputational damage. During investigations after the incident, the reviewers found that quite a number of middle managers knew about the issues and potential risks associated with the upgrade. However, the severity of the issues was not understood by senior management early enough for them to intervene before the major failure.

The organisation had a 'good news culture' in which people were afraid to raise issues to management. Some were told, 'Don't bring problems, bring solutions'. When people raised issues, they were told they were 'naysayers' who didn't have a 'can-do' attitude. While the exact conversations and decision-making processes are unknown, you can imagine that the people who knew may have been pressured by peers to soften the message so as not to get into trouble, and the senior managers may not have heard the warnings and pushed ahead to meet the IT upgrade deadlines.

What people in the mainstream or those with power often do not realise is that simply having a contrary view can be frightening. Sharing this contrary view incurs the risk of being criticised, judged or excluded. If you have a highly agreeable nature as described in Chapter 4, it feels like an extremely high risk.

Have you ever held back from sharing your views because it was different to everyone else's views? As a leader, how have you supported productive conversations with alternative views?

Hiding parts of ourselves

Katrina Webb, Paralympic gold medallist, international speaker, leadership and personal mastery consultant, has minor cerebral palsy: unless she tells you, you don't notice that she has a slight tilt and limp when she walks.

Katrina didn't know that she had cerebral palsy until she was 18; she just knew something was wrong and she worked very hard to hide it. She would never wear her night leg brace when friends would stay the night and she would hide it somewhere so no one would find it. She told her parents not to tell anyone. To cover it up and prove that she was good enough, she worked extremely hard at school and sport, so much so that she got into the Australian Institute of Sport on a full scholarship in netball. It was only when she started at the institute that she discovered she had cerebral palsy. When she realised she could go to the Paralympic games, she had very mixed feelings:

> *I then realised I could go to the Paralympic Games, which was exciting, and it's super exciting now, and the best thing that ever happened to me at that time as an 18-year-old. It frightened me though, because it meant that I would have to come out and let everyone know there was something wrong. I didn't know how to do that.*

She had worked hard to keep her cerebral palsy hidden, and it took her a lot of courage to let people know. This is despite cerebral palsy being the most common physical disability in childhood: approximately 34,000 people have cerebral palsy in Australia. Eventually, she recognised that it felt a lot better to be open than to be the hidden version of herself.

In addition to being open about her disability, another challenge for her was that her disability is not noticeable unless you know about it. She commented:

People have this image of what disability looks like without realising – it's the unconscious, biased view that disability is a certain way. Then, I rock up, and they say, 'Whoa. That doesn't fit with what I thought disability was'. And so, there's this story: 'Well, I don't really fit in this category, because I'm not super-disabled, and I don't fit in that [able-bodied world] either. Where do I actually fit?' Once I realised 90 per cent of disabilities are hidden and invisible, I gave myself permission [to be completely myself].

Keeping quiet about something that doesn't fit the mainstream and covering it up is something that people with disabilities or mental illness may do, especially if their condition is mild and unrecognisable to the eye. It could even be a characteristic of yours that you feel is a weakness.

As explored in Chapter 3, however, 'covering' has a personal cost and limits our ability to contribute our best. Katrina's story is one of courageously embracing her full self and excelling in her own unique way.

When have you felt you had to hide parts of yourself? What was the cost and what did you do about it? As a leader, how do you create an environment in which people do not need to hide?

Addressing power imbalances

I once worked with a senior leadership team led by a general manager – let's call him Ben – who was a respected senior leader with deep knowledge of his field and complex problem-solving abilities. Ben and his very skilled and experienced senior team had an offsite planning day that I was asked to facilitate.

Something I noticed early on was that whenever a team member made a suggestion or answered a question posed by the group, most of the team members would glance over at Ben. To me, it seemed like they were looking for his endorsement. Ben was also asked the most questions, as if the team wanted his answers, not their peers'.

Ben and I spoke about this dynamic during the break. After the break, he tried asking the team questions to gain input from them, making sure that everyone in the team had an opportunity to speak, including the quieter members. The team still looked at Ben for approval of their ideas, however, and some sounded like they were saying what they thought he would like to hear. At the end of this session, when he shared his thoughts with the team, some members looked disappointed that what he said was different to what they had said.

When we debriefed again, Ben shared his frustration that he was not getting the most from his talented and experienced team. I had a hunch about what might be going on, so I shared: 'Ben, I think people believe you have all the answers already. You're respected for your intelligence and knowledge, and you do have clear views on some topics. Even when you asked a question, it was as if what you said at the end was the only correct answer. It looks like it's hard for the team to speak up about anything that counters your views'.

I also shared specific examples of when I noticed this dynamic, and Ben began to see the issue more clearly. He finally said, 'I don't want this to continue. I have a talented team and I need their input and for them to have more ownership. Some of the upcoming organisational changes will be really challenging and I don't have all the answers for that. What should I do?' As soon as he said that, I realised that he wasn't sharing enough about his worries with his team. I suggested that he start the next session by sharing how he was feeling and asking for the team's help.

It was an approach Ben had not taken before, so he felt vulnerable. But when he did, the reaction and the shift in the team energy was palpable. A few people started to suggest ideas, then another few walked up to the whiteboard to draw up a way to think about the issues, and they talked to each other, rather than to Ben. A handful of team members even went back to the whiteboard after the day had finished and continued the discussion. The dynamic had changed dramatically.

Even though there was no toxicity in the team, people had been holding back their ideas in fear of judgement by the person who had the highest rank and greatest perceived knowledge. Ben's transparency about his concerns and his vulnerability allowed the team to see him as human, not as powerful or as a person to be feared. It took some awareness and courage on his part to break this dynamic, but the reward of unlocking the talent in the team was well worth the effort.

The #metoo movement is a global example of people with lower rank raising their voices to those who have misused their power. A large group of women stood up against perpetrators of abuse, including a group of female actors who called out the offences of the once-untouchable film producer Harvey Weinstein. Their collective voice helped to counter the struggles of power imbalance.

Individual women who were abused often feel powerless, as they are not taken seriously or listened to. When #metoo was tweeted by American actress Alyssa Milano around noon on 15 October 2017, the hashtag was used more than 200,000 times by the end of the day and tweeted more than 500,000 times by October 16. On Facebook, the hashtag was used by more than

4.7 million people in 12 million posts during the first 24 hours. Since this time, abuse allegations have been taken more seriously, and I would hope that victims of abuse (women, men and children) feel more comfortable, even if only slightly, to come forward.

What have you done when you have felt unsafe to speak up? If you are a leader, what have you done to first notice a lack of safety and then address it?

~

You can see that power dynamics have an enormous effect on whether people remain hidden or not. Some of the most extroverted people can go into hiding in some situations because they feel powerless. The key challenge is for those in the mainstream and those with higher rank to become more aware of their power and impact.

Chapter 7

Holding yourself back

Whatever the contributing traits, upbringing, conditioning or power dynamics may be, the bigger issue is that being quiet is perceived as negative and a disadvantage in the workplace, rather than as a quality to appreciate.

People can remain quiet and hidden because they hold themselves back, and this is often the most difficult issue to address. Even if they are in an environment that presents no barriers to thriving, a lifetime of experiences of being marginalised can weigh on them. Most people don't even realise that they have been absorbing messages that make them feel small. And because they don't notice these messages that are playing on repeat in their heads, they believe it is just who they are, and do not question them.

The messages we hear

Whenever I openly share that I am an introvert when facilitating a workshop or presenting to a group, I usually have one or more people come up and say, 'Surely you're not an introvert!' A few of my Quietly Powerful leader interviewees said that they have also experienced this reaction. I never used to be bothered by it, but I realised after some reflection that there's an unintended putdown in that comment. There's an implied assumption that an introvert would or could not behave in the way that I did in front of groups – that it's a surprise that an introvert could do what I do. You could also interpret it as implying that there is something wrong with being an introvert, especially if the comment is made in a condescending tone, as if to say, 'Surely you're not one of them?'

Where workplaces or social circles favour the alpha, dominant, extrovert styles, the opposite – non-alpha, feminine and quieter approaches – are not considered valuable. If you have heard some comments such as the ones below in performance conversations or on selection panels, you know that there is a bias:

- 'She's too quiet, she needs to speak up and promote herself more.' Meaning: being a quiet achiever is not good enough.
- 'He delivers, but is not ready to be a leader;, he needs more confidence and executive presence.' Meaning: the appearance of confidence = competence.
- 'She didn't interview very well. She didn't sell herself enough.' Meaning: selling herself is the most important skill for the job.

These comments, while they may seem appropriate, reinforce bias towards outspoken, confident-looking types. Rarely are there comments around the need for people to be less outspoken, more humble and to listen better.

Michelle Grocock, Executive General Manager, Internal Audit at National Australia Bank, spoke of a time earlier in her career when she thought she had to be like her extroverted colleagues:

There are a few moments of truth in terms of my leadership style. One of those was working for a couple of individuals, a couple of guys I really respected, and thought were fantastic; they were very extroverted. I fell into that trap we all fall into, of thinking success is trying to look like them. And I tried. I failed. So many mistakes at that point in time [involved] trying to replicate something that's not me.

Brad Chan, CEO of Banna Property Group and the Founder of Haymarket HQ, also had experiences of thinking that he needed to be an extrovert to be successful. He said:

I think one of the challenges I experienced earlier in my career, and particularly in working in a corporate environment, was I used to think that you needed to be an extrovert to move up and to be successful. And I think making that presumption is a bit disheartening when you're younger because you sort of thought, 'Well, how am I ever going to achieve this, where I have to be something that I'm not?' And I'm glad it's an incorrect assumption, and I know that now.

Below are other comments I've heard or read that put down being quiet, introverted, feminine or soft:

- 'They are quiet and introverted *but* have been successful.' Meaning: it's a surprise that a quiet person has been successful.
- 'I'm lucky I'm an extrovert.' Meaning: we're unlucky we're introverts.
- 'Don't be such a girl.' Meaning: girls are not favoured – with connotations of being soft and weak.
- 'Don't look so serious – smile!' (Said when a quiet person is in deep thought.) Meaning: deep thinking and seriousness are not valued.

Sometimes such comments are disguised as light-hearted jokes. We laugh, but if we identify with what's been described, a part of us feels mocked. Many of these comments and jokes involve stereotypes, too. They are not true for everyone and not true all the time. People who may appear quiet can be talented social connectors, skilled presenters and superb leaders, comedians and actors when they choose to be.

Internalised marginalisation

The biggest problem is the internalisation of these negative and subtle messages, which make us feel inferior.

Internalised marginalisation – sometimes called 'internalised oppression' or 'introjection' – is a psychological state of living with marginalisation even when the external marginalisation is gone. A person who has internalised marginalisation has accepted their learned unimportance and inferiority as the truth.

As quiet professionals, this internalisation can present as either hiding the qualities that are deemed as inferior to get ahead, or hiding in positions that keep us invisible.

We are told that we need to be more confident, to speak up more and promote ourselves. We are sent to development programs where techniques are taught, often in an extrovert-biased setting. For quieter professionals, this can result in feeling like there's something wrong with us and that we need fixing. Even if we manage to fake it for a while, it affects our confidence. Sadly, some of the well-meaning advice does more damage than good.

With so much to fix, our inner critic gets louder and harsher. At times the inner critic takes over and anxiety becomes constant. This causes us to retreat into our shells under pressure, or snap when we can't hold our frustrations in. We are misunderstood: we're too reserved when we retreat and too aggressive when we speak up. We can't win! Then, the inner critic grows, and the cycle continues.

This is one of the reasons why many quiet professionals, especially women and people in the minority, have a feeling of 'not being good enough' and can be hesitant to put themselves forward for promotions or new or senior roles. It can also be why people suffer from the imposter syndrome, believing they don't deserve the role they have been appointed to, and that they will be 'found out'.

Do you ever hear a voice in your head that tells you that you are 'not good enough' because of your characteristics? Do you find it easier to point to your weaknesses than to your strengths? What messages might you have internalised from your upbringing, societal biases or unintentional putdowns by others?

Playing the blame game

Professionals in minority groups or a lower rank – often women, people of colour, LGBTIQ+ people, people with disabilities, introverts and people in junior ranks – get told to 'be more confident', 'lean in', 'be more visible', 'promote yourself', 'build your personal brand' and 'develop an executive presence'. Essentially, they are told to fit the mould of the mainstream leader.

While some of these skills can be useful, the constant barrage of feedback that we need to improve or change ourselves can feed our inner critic; it adds to our already-undermining internalised marginalisation. When we're not able to fit the mould of the mainstream leader, we believe we're not good enough, and blame ourselves.

We start by blaming our natural traits, such as our introversion, emotionality or feminine qualities (for example, being too soft and sensitive). We may blame our genes and upbringing or blame some of our disadvantages.

We may also feel that 'they' don't understand. It feels unfair that we are not getting recognised for our hard work and capabilities. We might cycle between telling ourselves, 'If only I were X I could…' and saying, 'If only they could understand…'

This is how we can get stuck.

Holding yourself back

The music you were born to play, that is uniquely yours, is silenced as you try to fit in by playing others' music, or when others expect or coerce you to play their music. Worse, you may have forgotten what your music sounds like. You may have to go on an inner journey to uncover the music you were born to play.

A few can touch the magic string, and noisy fame is proud to win them: Alas for those that never sing, but die with all their music in them!
—Oliver Wendell Holmes Senior, from the poem 'The Voiceless'

When you realise you are stuck in this pattern and you acknowledge that it is not working for you, it's an opportunity to make a conscious choice to either continue or to let it go and follow another path. Rather than remaining quiet and hidden, you can choose to use your quiet nature as your advantage.

This is the final reason why someone may be quiet: to deliberately use their quieter style effectively. Unlike the other reasons, it is an empowering use of our quiet nature, and that is Quietly Powerful.

~

Being quiet and hidden isn't necessarily about introversion; human beings are so much more complex than introversion and extroversion. Many of us are a mix of both and much more. Some of us – like myself – are fortunate or unfortunate enough to have many of the above elements to deal with. As a Japanese woman with an introvert preference and conflict- and attention-avoidant tendencies, and often being a minority in the Australian business world, it has been quite a challenge to find my voice and be heard.

Others have a different combination of attributes and their own unique set of challenges. A few Asian men have shared with me that being taken seriously has been difficult for them, as men are expected to be 'strong', 'confident' and 'outspoken' in the Western context, where the opposite is often the stereotype of Asian men. Many of them also have a long-standing cultural conditioning of valuing humility, so self-promotion and being the centre of attention not only feels awkward, but as if they are going against their values.

If they fit the stereotype, they are not seen as leader-like. If they don't fit the stereotype, they are either assumed to fit the stereotype and are overlooked anyway, or may be seen as 'self-obsessed'. This is a similar challenge to 'assertive' women who don't fit the feminine stereotype and are called 'aggressive'.

Once you understand the complex mix of reasons for feeling quietly disempowered, you can choose to work on how you can thrive using your quiet strengths, which I will share in Part IV. First, though, let's consider why organisations overlook and underutilise Quietly Powerful talent.

Part III

Disregard for quiet talent

THE ISSUES AROUND hidden talent are not just due to an individual's predispositions and conditioning. So how did it happen that organisations and society at large disregard quiet talent and assume that they are not leadership material? It is strange because there are people who say their quiet leaders have been the best to work for. There's a mismatch between what we say we want in our leaders and the leaders who succeed and progress up the ladder.

Part III explores the key contributors to this mismatch, including our irrational unconscious biases, the resulting biased systems and processes and outdated beliefs about leadership.

Chapter 8

Biased and fooled

Thanks to all the efforts in diversity and inclusion in organisations, the term unconscious bias is now well known and many of us know that human beings are biased. What we may not realise, due to the unconscious nature of these biases, is the extent to which we are biased and in what ways we are biased. Even people who have studied unconscious bias may not realise that organisations routinely overlook potential Quietly Powerful leaders because they don't fit the traditional style of leadership. The following are some of these biases and how they contribute to the mismatch between the types of leaders we want and those we actually choose.

Strong leadership = dominance

A senior female leader, whom I had never met, wrote to me via LinkedIn out of sheer frustration. She had a solid track record but was unsuccessful securing a role she had applied for. She was told by the recruiter that she was unsuccessful because the hiring manager was looking for a 'strong leader'. She wrote in her message, 'I think they were looking for that [a dominating style of leader] because it is their current workplace culture. They fight, they push each other around...'

In the mind of the hiring manager, strong leadership meant being dominant and outspoken.

This bias has been well researched. Lindred Greer from Stanford University, Murat Tarakci and Patrick Groenen from the Rotterdam School of Management undertook research on how effective people are at recognising good leadership. It was based on an exercise of choosing a list of items they could use to survive after a plane crash had left them in the desert, then comparing that to the answers of a wilderness expert. When asked to choose a leader in the group after participants were told who the most qualified person was, there was still roughly a 50 per cent chance that they would choose the leader who was less competent, but 'taller, louder, or more confident.' This same exercise has been conducted for years, with similar outcomes.

Dr Tomas Chamorro-Premuzic's book, *Why do so Many Incompetent Men become Leaders? (and how to fix it)*, also raises the concern that we equate overconfidence and self-absorption as charismatic and leader-like. On the flipside, when we meet potential leaders who are humble, quiet and may not appear confident, we judge very quickly and unconsciously that they aren't leadership material.

Unfortunately, we also have additional cognitive biases, such as the confirmation bias, that cause us to select data that confirms our beliefs. For example, when we form a positive impression of the charismatic person, we see what is leader-like in them and miss things that should be warning signs. When we form a lukewarm impression of the quieter, less confident-looking person, we assume these are signs that equal lacking in competence. This can lead to discounting what they say and failing to ask the right questions to appreciate them. We are fooled by our first impressions.

Confidence = competence

Because of this belief that a strong leader looks confident, we are regularly told that confidence is the key to success. Many articles outline the need to appear confident, and this is especially directed at women. Lack of confidence is often used as the reason why women don't go for promotions, why they don't speak up or why they don't promote themselves. Many women are sent to leadership programs that involve building and demonstrating confidence and learning presentation skills, influencing skills and interviewing skills.

I've had plenty of well-meaning managers, mentors and teachers tell me to 'be more confident', but it doesn't help. In fact, it's telling me that I'm not confident enough to be good enough, which makes me feel worse.

Research described by Jack Nasher in his *HBR* article 'To Seem More Competent, Be More Confident' shows, unfortunately, that a confident appearance does in fact cause people to think they are more competent and there are major problems with this.

Firstly, people who look like they are confident are not always confident. You may know people who look and speak confidently, but when they are given corrective feedback, they get defensive, aggressive or they shut down. Truly confident people are able to take feedback, discern what's useful, admit that they make mistakes and that they will work on themselves. Truly confident people can be strong *and* vulnerable.

The danger is that leaders who only appear confident can have their insecurities leak out in dysfunctional ways. In the most serious cases, these leaders who are unaware or don't acknowledge their insecurities, may try to cover things up through various means. You may have seen behaviours such as:

- Dominating over others so they cannot be a threat
- Using fear to keep people under control

- Not listening to feedback, being defensive or even attacking the messenger as it threatens their confident sense of self
- An inability to listen to ideas that are not their own or different to their own
- An inability to show vulnerability or apologise for mistakes
- Blaming others for problems and not taking ownership for any part of the problem
- No or only a superficial demonstration of humility
- Displaying an inability to give credit to or develop others.

It is possible that these leaders have narcissistic tendencies. Psychologist, Dr Jeremy Dean, founder and author of PsyBlog, says that narcissists feel superior to others but aren't necessarily satisfied with themselves. They have a desire to be admired by others and can easily become aggressive and angry when they aren't. People who have high self-esteem see value in themselves but do not see themselves as more valuable than others.

Secondly, emphasising the importance of appearing confident can result in teams and organisations with arrogant, hubristic or narcissistic leaders who don't listen to others and think they have all the answers, believe they are invincible or lack empathy. The confident 'show' that they put on in the interview could be a toned-down version of their arrogance. Hubris can not only disengage people, but it can lead to poor decisions and disasters such as those we have seen through the global financial crisis, company failures and ethical lapses.

Research by David Dunning and Justin Kruger, social psychologists at Cornell University, shows that the least competent people are often the most overconfident about their own abilities, and the most competent often underestimate their abilities. Their explanation of this pattern is that when someone is incompetent, they lack the metacognitive skills that enable them to tell how poorly they are performing. Aristotle's quote 'The more you know, the more you know you don't know' plays out.

In organisations where appearing confident is valued, leaders may fail to show their vulnerabilities and refuse to admit their lack of knowledge or mistakes. This behaviour can be just as damaging to organisations as hubris, because mistakes are hidden and the blame game becomes the norm, which wastes valuable time and energy.

Thirdly, when confidence is mistaken for competence, organisations pay the price by making incompetent hires. By being seduced by the confident exterior and failing to dig deeper, organisations miss the opportunity to hire, retain or promote highly competent individuals who don't appear confident. Some people are quietly confident and, as already discussed, there may also be gender and cultural differences in how confidence is presented.

Most of us have seen the damage caused by overconfident individuals or by people who appear confident without the substance. Still, we are drawn to and are impressed by these people. It is an emotional reaction, not a rational one.

Mesmerised by charisma

Think of the last time you had a meeting, or were at a conference and a charismatic CEO or senior leader walked into the room. What happened? Everyone went quiet, smiled as they walked past, watched every move and listened to every word they said, right?

Have you ever noticed that when charismatic leaders speak, people hang on to every word they say, but when you write the words down, they are very simple, not very insightful or are full of impressive-sounding jargon? Sometimes simple messages are important to call people to action, but if they're full of clichés and jargon, why do people still fall for them?

A phenomenon known as the 'awestruck effect' has been researched and describes someone being awestruck by charismatic leaders, heroes and entertainers to such an extent that they lose their capacity to think rationally. As a result, they can be easily manipulated. Worse, they let them get away with abusing their power, either because they idolise them so much and believe they can do no wrong, or because they are too afraid to call them out when they misbehave.

I wonder how many people were fooled due to the awestruck effect by the likes of executives at Enron before its collapse and Catholic priests and senior cardinals who committed or overlooked sexual abuse. I'm sure there are many other cases where we have been awestruck and not looked past the style or positional title.

Unfortunately, charisma can also mask narcissistic and 'psychopathic' tendencies. Research conducted by Nicole Mead at the University of Melbourne showed that people who crave power and attention are more likely to turn narcissistic when they gain power. So, there is real danger in being awestruck by charismatic leaders.

Grant, Gino and Hofmann's paper, 'Reversing the Extraverted Leadership Advantage: The role of employee proactivity', refers to an online survey of 1,500 senior leaders earning at least six-figure salaries that found 65 per cent saw introversion as a negative quality in terms of leadership. The authors explain that extroverts are often perceived as more effective because of a 'halo effect'. These leaders match the prototypes of charismatic leaders that dominate both (Western and Eastern cultures) and are especially prevalent in business.

There is also an assumption here that you have to be extroverted to be charismatic. According to the *Oxford English Dictionary*, charisma is defined as: 1) Compelling attractiveness or charm that can inspire devotion in others; and 2) A divinely conferred power or talent.

Many Quietly Powerful leaders are accomplished public speakers and often described as charismatic in their own way. Off stage, however, you may be surprised to meet a shy, quiet person who prefers to speak with you one on one. They are naturally quiet individuals with skills, presence and positioning that they have developed over years. What's different about Quietly Powerful leaders is that their charisma is not self-focused or about attention seeking. We feel their presence and authenticity.

Attention seekers and takers

When we are time poor and under pressure, we are particularly prone to missing things as we rely on default thinking to be efficient, and default thinking can be riddled with biases.

We rely too much on first impressions. It's like when you're scanning through social media: the colourful pictures or the catchy titles grab your attention. Whether the article or item is fake news, has limited substance or is just a copy of someone else's idea, doesn't seem to matter. We simply gravitate to them and take the ideas on without thinking.

We are also plagued by short attention spans due to time pressure, being busy and a world of other distractions. It is easier to focus on what is visible in front of us and it takes a lot to attract and retain our attention. So, the people who do capture our attention, whether it's because they are entertaining, charming or smooth-talking, get a tick before they are properly assessed.

This tendency has resulted in a lot of focus on self-promotion, visibility, personal brand and image in the workplace. These are not necessarily bad, but they do reflect more on what's on the surface and less on what's behind the image. Quality and substance may not get the credit they deserve.

Quietly Powerful leaders can be less visible because they don't tend to actively self-promote. Their work is usually more visible than they are because they are more focused on the work and its purpose and less on their own personal branding or profile.

Have you ever been disappointed by a product that didn't live up to the marketing hype? You wouldn't just rely on the fancy marketing brochures to make your decision when buying something of high value, would you? I'm sure you would do your research, ask experts and friends you trust and look at recommendations from trusted sources.

Somehow, we don't tend to do this level of homework and investigation when it comes to selecting leaders. We may be over-confident in our ability to judge people's character and suitability for leadership roles.

In addition, we unconsciously value comfort and look for a 'cultural fit', for people who are 'on the same page' and are 'like-minded', people we get along with, people who look, sound and feel like us. With the pressure to get results, it is natural to choose the usual suspects. Over time, however, we miss the opportunities that different styles and thinking bring to teams and organisations, as described in many papers such as 'Delivering through Diversity' by McKinsey.

We select leaders who appear leader-like, based on what we've been comfortable with in the past. During the presidential election of 2016, some people in the US said Hillary Clinton was not 'presidential enough'. Well, of course, she didn't look anything like the previous 44 presidents, so there was a mismatch between what people were used to and what they were seeing.

This is exactly the fast, subconscious-based System 1 thinking described by Daniel Kahneman in *Thinking, Fast and Slow*. We tend to go with what we know and believe that what we see is all there is, without thinking too hard or making the effort to investigate properly.

The problem is that senior leaders promote the wrong leaders because the more self-centred 'takers' tend to be better self-promoters, according to Adam Grant, author of *Give and Take*. In other words, decision-makers are more easily fooled by the smooth-talkers than they might think. Unfortunately, when decisions are made with System 1 thinking, the result is that attention seekers and the usual suspects win.

What we say we want versus who we choose

We say that good leadership shows up in many forms. Books and articles are written about the benefit of and need for different leadership styles and behaviours. However, often unconsciously, we keep choosing the traditional 'strong' leaders – maybe because there is a misconception that these leaders will protect and look after us.

Leaders who listen

We say we want leaders who listen but it's people who don't listen who still get promoted. The outspoken, louder people in a room are seen as 'leader-like' and able to take charge. They are noticed and talked about in promotion discussions, regardless of the quality of ideas they share or the effectiveness of their listening.

Just about every employee survey conducted in organisations raises 'communication' as an issue. There is an element of people wanting more relevant information from their leaders, but it is also about the lack of connection and listening. People who work for leaders who genuinely listen, like the Quietly Powerful leader interviewees, feel valued, engaged and want to contribute their best to the team and organisation. We all know the difference between feeling listened to and not listened to, and how that experience impacts our level of trust and respect for that person.

Leaders with humility

We say we want leaders with humility while telling people to be 'more confident' and promote themselves.

Humility has been identified as a powerful leadership attribute by authors such as Robert Greenleaf in his book, *Servant Leadership* in 1977 and Jim Collins in his book, *Good to Great* in 2001. The concept of humility in leadership and its positive effects is not new. Most people appreciate leaders who show that they don't have all the answers or acknowledge when they have made a mistake.

If we want leaders with humility, why then do we tell people to self-promote and lean-in to get ahead in their careers? Quiet professionals, women, people in the minority continue to get taught the power pose – how to look confident – and are told to stop apologising.

Leaders showing vulnerability

We say we want leaders to show some vulnerability, while vulnerability and emotionality are seen as weaknesses.

Brené Brown, research professor in Social Work at the University of Houston, debunked the myths about vulnerability in her books and TED talks. One of these myths is that vulnerability is weakness. She asks the question, 'Vulnerability is the emotion that we experience during times of uncertainty, risk and emotional exposure. Can you give me a single example of courage that you've experienced or seen in others that did not require experiencing vulnerability?' No one can give examples of vulnerability without courage.

It takes courage and strength to show vulnerability, yet most leaders shy away from sharing that they are unsure and have doubts. They worry about being perceived as lacking confidence, competence and professionalism, given the bias discussed earlier. In her 2019 talk in Melbourne, Brené said, 'If you don't do feelings, you shouldn't be a leader.'

Humble leaders who listen and show some vulnerability exist already, but they are overshadowed by overconfident leaders who dominate and maintain the appearance of being strong.

Bill Taylor, co-founder of Fast Company, wrote in his article, 'If Humility Is So Important, Why Are Leaders So Arrogant?':

> *We live in a world where ego gets attention but modesty gets results. Where arrogance makes headlines but humility makes*

a difference. Which means that all of us, as leaders or aspiring leaders, face questions of our own: Are we confident enough to stay humble?

More recently, a *Wall Street Journal* article by Sue Shellenbarger, 'The Best Bosses are Humble Bosses', indicated that some organisations are pushing to promote people who don't seek the spotlight.

Are we ready to put in the effort to find people with genuine humility and see past the first impressions and visible marketing?

A political leader who seems to have cut through the challenge of not fitting the leader-like mould is New Zealand Prime Minister, Jacinda Ardern. In the early days of her leadership, people were concerned or cast doubt on her abilities for reasons such as her age, her pregnancy and giving birth while in the role. She certainly does not look or act like a leader that most of us are used to.

On 15 March 2019, after the horrific attack in a mosque in Christchurch, Ardern said that it was: 'one of New Zealand's darkest days,' and that: 'New Zealand is united in grief'. The way in which she united the country when it could easily have been divided, how she genuinely cared for those grieving, how she acted swiftly on their gun laws were leadership actions that so many around the world watched in awe.

It was as if people were woken up to the possibility of a different kind of leader, someone who shows emotion and compassion more readily. The praise that she received from around the world as a strong leader who shows kindness and warmth was in stark contrast to the image of the traditional 'strong' leader we had held.

Jacinda Ardern herself has publicly stated, 'One of the criticisms I've faced over the years is that I'm not aggressive enough or assertive enough or maybe somehow, because I'm empathetic, it means I'm weak. I totally rebel against that. I refuse to believe that you cannot be both compassionate and strong.'

So, are we ready to embrace a range of different styles in our leaders, including those who may be quieter, understated and humble? Are we ready to embrace leaders who listen, have humility and show vulnerability?

Chapter 9

Outdated beliefs about leadership

We are still emotionally attached to confident, charismatic and heroic leadership because we haven't updated our beliefs about what leadership is for. As a result, we tend to expect too much of individual leaders. It made sense in the context of military operations, emergencies and in the industrial era, for command and control to be the most effective and efficient approach to leadership.

But the world has changed, and command and control is no longer the most effective in a range of different contexts such as knowledge-based work, need for innovation, constant change and uncertainty, digitisation and broader information access. We need to think about the purpose of leadership in these different contexts.

What is leadership for?

In a workshop with emerging female leaders, we discussed which qualities, behaviours and mindsets of leaders stood out as being effective. We did a quick sort of these items into what fit the typical 'alpha' style versus those which did not. While I recognise the distinction between 'alpha', 'non-alpha' and 'other' was intuitive rather than scientific, it was interesting to see that the 'non-alpha' board had at least 50 per cent more items than the 'alpha' board. Many 'non-alpha' behaviours stood out, such as listening, caring, being supportive, providing opportunities and being interested.

We then discussed what leadership was actually for, rather than what it should look like. The group considered ideas along the lines of 'the main purpose of leadership is to unite and inspire a group of people to move forward and get things done.'

One of the frameworks which helped this conversation was James Scouller's work. In his book, *The Three Levels of Leadership*, Scouller defines leadership as a process, not a person and that there are four dimensions involved.

> *Leadership is a process that involves: setting a purpose and direction which inspires people to combine and work towards willingly; paying attention to the means, pace and quality of progress towards the aim; and upholding group unity and individual effectiveness throughout.*

If the function of leadership exists to address these four dimensions, how they are addressed will vary depending on the person, the team, the organisation, system and the situation and environment. *There is no one way to lead.* Scouller also suggests that one person cannot do everything. The individual leader's job, then, is to ensure that function of leadership exists.

In this workshop, some were relieved to hear that they didn't have to know everything as a leader. Others discussed how our natural strengths can be valuable for different aspects of leadership. Some leaders motivate through charisma and others motivate through building ownership by stepping back (motivating purpose). Some have natural strengths around ensuring things get done (task progress) and others are naturally good at building great teams (group unity). The group found it difficult to identify leaders who possessed all four dimensions, but they knew of leaders who had people around them who were good at dimensions that weren't their own natural strengths.

Expecting too much of individual leaders

We idolise individual leaders who are successful and stand out. We love the idea of there being a special X-factor to success in leadership, business and life. Maybe this is due to our childhood memories of superheroes, the comfort of being looked after by our parents or the yearning to be looked after if we weren't cared for. There is a feeling within most of us that we expect individual leaders to fulfil these roles.

Peter Block, in his book *Stewardship: Choosing Service over Self Interest*, advocates replacing leadership – that is, the traditional hierarchical and patriarchal leadership – with stewardship. He explains that traditional leadership creates a dependency dynamic like a parent-child relationship where the leader, like a parent, knows better and has control. Those who are under their control, expect to be looked after and in doing so, give away power and control to the leader. Block says:

> *Our search for strong leadership expresses the desire for others to assume the ownership and responsibility for our group, our organisation, our society. The effect is to localise power, purpose and privilege in the one we call leader.*

Stewardship, on the other hand, creates a sense of ownership and responsibility for outcomes at every level of the organisation. It is an approach that empowers people such that adult-to-adult relationships and partnerships preside over the parent-child relationship. It requires all of us to step up rather than expect the individual leader to work things out for us. Block states that stewardship can only work:

> *When we choose service over self-interest, say we are willing to be deeply accountable without choosing to control the world around us. It requires a level of trust that we are not used to holding.*

The concept of stewardship proposed by Block encompasses how the whole system would need to change, including things like governance, management structures, compensation and more. However, it is also an invitation for all of us to assess how we may be contributing to the traditional patriarchal leadership paradigm both as followers and leaders. We have been expecting too much of individual leaders. As a result, we look for individuals who appear confident and able to take on such superhero roles, but we are often disappointed when we realise they are only human.

Scouller takes a similar view regarding those who are led in his article 'Why Don't We Get the Political Leaders We Need?' He said:

> *It's the readiness of the led that decides who can become their leader… and what they can achieve… otherwise they'll put new leaders on pedestals and expect them to produce wonders without raising a finger to help. When that happens, we set up leaders to fail because we're not recognising that leadership is a process that's always shared between leaders and so-called followers, who I'd prefer to call co-leaders.*

What is common across these concepts of Scouller, Greenleaf and Block is that leadership is about serving the collective and this cannot be performed by an individual. As the world becomes complex, inter-connected and inter-dependent, it is impossible to rely on one or a few leaders to solve problems such as climate change, waste, economic inequality, physical and cyber security. As organisations become disrupted and business models change, it is also impossible for one or a few leaders to change the culture and deep-seated mindsets in a meaningful way. Expecting individual leaders to fix the problems is unreasonable and increasingly dangerous – we need more leaders to emerge at every level.

Chapter 10

Biased systems and processes

With such biased and outdated thinking about leadership, it is no wonder organisational systems and processes are also biased. Organisations and leaders keep their diverse talent hidden and under-utilised, often without realising. Below are a few common organisational systems and processes that do not get the best out of your quiet talent.

Assessment and promotion

Even if organisations use blind CVs as a way of limiting unconscious bias based on names, the following assessment and promotion processes still make it difficult, if not impossible, for talented people to jump through the hoops if they don't appear traditionally leader-like.

- **Personality profiling** – intentionally or unintentionally, you may recruit, select or promote with particular personality profiles in mind. Even if it's not explicit, you may have an unconscious bias against certain profiles, especially for leadership roles. Extroversion and high dominance are traits that are perceived to be better for leadership, so you look for them regardless of the lack of evidence of such correlation. I have seen cases where potential candidates weren't shortlisted based on such personality profiles, having been assessed against the 'ideal' leadership profile.

- **Recruitment, selections and promotion interviews** – the interviewers may not be attentive or skilled enough to uncover talents of people who may not impress in the first ten seconds. Sometimes the most talented people take time to warm up. They may need an extra question or two along with good listening to share the depth of their expertise and substance. The quality of the interviewer's questions and interaction skills can help or hinder the talents from being revealed. Confirmation bias also kicks in such that the first impression may distort the interviewer's assessment.

- **Leadership assessment centres** – many assessment centres focus on group work, working quickly, speaking up, thinking on your feet and presenting after a short period to prepare. It's a pressure cooker situation which challenges people. However, it is biased against people who prefer to prepare with reading, research and reflection. A one- or two-day assessment centre only measures some of the important skills required for leadership but is treated as if it measures everything. How can someone's real talents and substance be uncovered when they are not given the opportunity to be so?

- **Leadership frameworks** – some leadership frameworks are skewed towards certain qualities, while others are more balanced, and leadership development programs may be inconsistent as a result. When it comes to assessment against the frameworks, some elements may get more weighting due to our cognitive biases.

- **Assessment conversations** – some conversations are regarded more for style, impressions and visibility rather than substance. Talented people are often overlooked despite their achievements, quality output, strong relationships with their teams and peers and influencing skills. This is either because they don't fit the usual leadership style or they were too busy delivering outcomes to worry about self-promotion.

- **Lack of feedback from the team** – leaders are appointed by their leaders and they rarely, if ever, receive feedback about their leadership effectiveness from their team. Some people keep getting promoted even though nobody wants to work for them, while other people don't get promoted even though their team love working for them and perform well under their guidance.

Stereotypes, assumptions and unconscious biases are systematically allowed to influence, if not determine, recruitment, selection and promotion decisions. Not only do talented people go unnoticed, they can lose their confidence, just like Sally in Chapter 1. Because of this damaged confidence, they are less likely to put their hands up again, in fear of having to go through the same experience. This is a way to maintain the status quo and limits progress on diversity at leadership levels.

Office environment

Another quiet professional I met at an event – let's call her Penny – spoke about a project she was involved in with a few other colleagues who liked to talk a lot. While Penny had useful knowledge, she was unable to contribute effectively as she was not given time to prepare and was often spoken over when she did try to contribute. She was also overwhelmed by the number of informal and formal meetings that took place. She felt she couldn't make sufficient progress on the project without some independent thinking and working time. In the end, she asked to be taken off the project as it was starting to affect her mental and emotional well-being.

While Penny received support from her manager to leave the project, she sensed an unspoken, underlying judgement that it was her fault that she was not resilient enough to deal with the project environment.

Some office environments do not cater for quiet space and thinking time. The popularity of open plan offices and flexi-desking grew out of the belief that it would increase collaboration and informal interaction while saving on office space. Thus, interaction is valued over thinking. Interestingly though, a new study has found that employees in open-plan offices spend 73 per cent less time in face-to-face interactions and email and messaging usage shot up by over 67 per cent.

In addition, more studies are showing the productivity cost of an open space working environment. A 2013 study based on a survey of 43,000 workers in the *Journal of Environmental Psychology*, concluded that the disadvantages of noise and distraction associated with open office plans outweighed the anticipated, but still unproven, benefits of increasing morale and productivity boosts from unplanned interactions.

If you are overwhelmed by noisy environments and are naturally more productive in quiet spaces, you can imagine the extra productivity loss!

Meetings and offsites

Another quiet professional – let's call her Deb – spoke about an offsite full of group activities followed by a 'get to know your colleagues speed dating' process, then drinks and dinner in the evening. Nothing was given to them to prepare, there was no time to think and reflect and no time to get away. Deb felt put on the spot and unable to contribute her knowledge or expertise in a useful way. She described it as 'traumatising' and was exhausted afterwards. When she described this experience with a colleague, she was told that it only happened occasionally and that she should get over it.

Like Deb, many quiet professionals dread going to team offsites where they would be with a large group of people, many of whom they don't know. This concern is often ignored and not much is designed in these offsites to support them in contributing more effectively.

There is also a common belief that brainstorming is the best way to come up with creative ideas. Brainstorming is a method used in many organisations, despite research showing that brainstorming groups produce fewer and poorer quality ideas than individuals working alone.

Think of the last brainstorming session you took part in. Did you find that a few people spoke more than the rest? Did you notice anyone who contributed an idea and it got shot down? How did this person behave after the idea got shot down? Did you have ideas you wanted to contribute but didn't get a chance because you ran out of time? Did you have ideas that you held back from sharing because you were worried they might be regarded as silly or because the boss or someone senior was in the room? Have you noticed that the group coalesced around a few ideas (groupthink) – possibly the ideas of the most senior people in the group – and ignored others?

Adrian Furnham, Professor of Psychology and Director of Business Psychology Unit at University College London, wrote in *The Brainstorming Myth* that research from as early as 1958 rejects the claim that brainstorming is an effective way of generating ideas. He identifies three processes which make brainstorming ineffective:

1. **Social loafing** – the group context that enables individuals to make less effort

2. **Evaluation apprehension** – the fear of suggesting ideas which might make one look foolish
3. **Production blocking** – only one group member can suggest an idea in any moment.

Some progressive organisations are using the benefit of quiet thinking spaces and the power of groups by using new techniques. Examples include:

- brainwriting, where the group members write their ideas down individually first, then share with the group in a structured way

- hybrid brainstorming, a structured process involving individual thinking time, writing ideas on Post-it Notes and individually adding to others' ideas by passing the Post-it Notes around the table.

Many workplaces continue to ignore these findings, however, and run brainstorming at offsites, workshops and meetings without adjusting for deep thinkers or to avoid groupthink.

Are we ready to challenge our default ways of working and the systems we have put in place that may have been adequate in the past but are contributing to wasting our quiet talent?

Chapter 11

Time for an update

I'm not advocating for the replacement of outspoken leaders with Quietly Powerful leaders. That would be a shame, as we would miss the energy and entertainment, and sometimes these dominant forces are needed for radical change or during emergency situations. However, the concept of the superhero individual leader that attracts attention – often called the 'natural leader' – is simply incomplete and outdated.

We need to expand the definition of good leadership and understand that it can look, sound and feel different to that which we have worshipped in the past. It is about embracing the yin and yang, the feminine and masculine, the reflection and action, the listening and speaking and the substance and style.

Imagine the talent pool that would open up if we were more skilled at seeing below the surface and if we assessed leadership potential based on performance and capability and not by perceived capability proxied by a confident appearance.

If more of us – regardless of personality, conditioning or being in the mainstream or minority – accessed the state of Quietly Powerful, and used it as a strength in leadership, we could then lift the quality of leadership to meet the challenges of the increasingly complex world we live in.

Additionally, to attain a position in leadership, qualified leaders and potential leaders should focus on doing the work of leadership rather than self-promotion. We could then stop appointing the toxic, narcissistic and self-interested leaders we regularly see today.

Failure to notice

In my presentations, after discussing our perception of quiet people, I often ask the audience if they know anyone who doesn't say a lot but has enormous impact when they do. A lot of hands go up. I also remind the audience of times when they may have felt someone's calming presence before they spoke and many can usually think of examples.

We don't always notice these quiet powers among the noise, busyness and distractions. Despite how effective they are, these Quietly Powerful leaders can remain hidden unless enough of us are observant and attentive.

Oscar Trimboli, as mentioned in Chapter 3, was told by one of his managers that he could add enormous value due to his ability to listen and observe. It was his ability to listen to the conversation in a room, sometimes with disparate ideas – and ask a critical question to the group – that would shift thinking to another level. He recalls:

> *Tracey noticed in a meeting the observations I made stopped the room. Afterwards, she took me aside and said, 'You didn't realise the impact you had on the room, did you?' 'No,' I said. She replied, 'At about the 35-minute mark of a 90-minute meeting, you made an observation about how the group was interacting and the group didn't actually notice that about themselves, but it moved the group forward because they were stuck.'*

Oscar believes that Quietly Powerful leaders have observational curiosity. They're not just observing or curious about the dialogue and the content being discussed, but they're also looking at the interplay between people in the room. They're listening to orientations of language and where the coalitions are. They're connecting what's happening in the room with what's happening outside in the broader business and the market. They may not say much, but what they do say is based on these observations and connections that others may have missed.

Think of effective leaders who use the power of quiet effectively and intentionally. The power of quiet – whether it shows up as stillness, mindfulness, listening, observation, stepping back, slowing down, reflection, deep and creative thinking or connecting the dots – is underutilised and undervalued as a leadership strength. Diana Renner and Steven D'Souza called these 'negative capabilities' and highlighted their importance in leadership in their book, *Not Doing*. I love that.

The best leaders are great listeners. They deliberately take a quieter approach to building relationships, influencing, selling ideas, solving problems, speaking, facilitating, coaching and having difficult conversations.

Having interviewed 29 Quietly Powerful leaders from a variety of fields at the time of writing, it's clear to me that these leaders exist, and they are highly effective. Every time I spoke with a Quietly Powerful leader, I wished I'd worked for them earlier in my career. Luckily, I did work with one – Steve Hodgkinson. He was the client manager on one of the best consulting projects I've ever been involved in.

I've also had numerous messages from people, via email or LinkedIn, tell me that some of the best leaders they've worked for have been the quieter ones. For example:

> *I worked for one year with a supervisor who exhibited many of the traits of the listener leader you described, and it was one of the happiest years of my career.*

> *The best leader I have ever worked for was a woman… [who] was quiet, strong and able to motivate in the most pleasant way I have ever encountered in my many years in management.*

On the world stage, Angela Merkel is often referred to as having a quiet power. She has been the Chancellor of Germany since 2005 and has led her country through the global financial crisis and Europe's economic crises. For many, she has represented the stability in an unstable and chaotic world. She is a quantum chemist who is so private that even the German people do not know a lot about her. Her image is one of a safe pair of hands, trustworthy, straightforward and careful – she is Quietly Powerful, not because of her style, but because of her substance and actions.

Zen master Thich Nhat Hanh comes to mind as a Quietly Powerful leader. He is a global spiritual leader, poet and peace activist, revered throughout the world for his powerful messages on mindfulness and peace. If you watch him speak, you can see that Thich Nhat Hanh is a quietly spoken, gentle and humble monk. In fact, he is a teacher who can teach without speaking. When asked about whether he will retire as a teacher, he answered:

> *Even if I don't give a Dharma talk, I like to join walking meditation, sitting meditation, eating in mindfulness and so on… You don't need to talk in order to teach. You need to live your life mindfully and deeply.*

He also teaches the importance of silence and the ability to hold a quiet space within ourselves:

> *Silence is essential. We need silence, just as much as we need air, just as much as plants need light. If our minds are crowded with words and thoughts, there is no space for us.*

We can feel the Quietly Powerful presence of these leaders. Their presence is calm, peaceful and one that many are drawn to. It's a feeling that many of us wish to have within ourselves.

Quietly Powerful is not an oxymoron.

Blind to the problem

Unfortunately, many people, particularly in senior positions, do not see the systemic biases or the impacts because they either naturally work well or have learned to work well in this system. Therefore quiet professionals and those in the minority feel disempowered, as they are told that they are the problem and they need to fix themselves to fit in.

Michael Kimmel, Professor of Sociology at Stony Brook University in New York, says in his TED talk, 'Why gender equality is good for everyone' that 'Privilege is invisible to those who have it.'

In the study, 'Vulnerability of Female Drivers Involved in Motor Vehicle Crashes', researchers found that the odds of a woman sustaining an injury while wearing a seatbelt were 47 per cent higher than for men wearing seatbelts. Until about 2000, air bags and seatbelts used to be designed primarily with men in mind. Just as safety features in cars have been made to keep the average man safe and not women, social, economic, employment and organisational systems are set up to advantage some and not others.

In the context of leadership potential and selection, not only is it an unlevel playing field, it's causing important leadership qualities to go unassessed and undervalued. The systemic biases are disadvantaging individuals as well as organisations. As Dr Tomas Chamorro-Premuzic says, incompetent men (and women) are still appointed through assessments rather than being assessed to be unsuitable.

We need to change the assessment criteria for leadership to put equal emphasis on listening, humility and thoughtfulness as we do on speaking, looking confident and giving quick, simple answers. Working environments need to be created where quiet, creative thinking and reflection are encouraged. These changes will allow Quietly Powerful leaders to emerge naturally as well as open up a larger pool of talent to contribute more fully in an organisation.

Some people will react to the change saying that it's not fair that people who have traditionally been overlooked are now given an advantage. I've had some people argue that my talks and articles are putting down good leaders who are extroverted and not-so-quiet. This is despite my efforts in saying how much I *do* value these colleagues and leaders and that they do have a lot to contribute but in a different way. My suggestion is simply a more balanced approach to leadership.

These are exactly the backlash responses you get when long-standing privileges are taken away from or are reduced for those who benefited from them without realising. This kind of backlash is very visible in the fields of gender equality and cultural and ethnic diversity.

When you're accustomed to privilege, equality feels like oppression.
—Source unknown

Most people would recognise the value of both styles of leadership from first-hand experience. If we can unite around the goal of enhancing the quality of leadership in organisations and society, there will be greater diversity in leadership styles, which will flow on to diversity and inclusion more broadly.

~

For individuals, it's time that quiet professionals see value in their quiet nature as a leadership strength, rather than see it as a disadvantage or a quality to hide. It's time they use it to lift the quality of leadership in organisations. Become aware of times when you are quietly disempowered and hiding and start choosing different responses to empower yourself.

Time for an update

For organisations, it's time to update leadership frameworks while also updating the beliefs and assumptions about what leadership looks, sounds and feels like. Go back to first principles and ask:

- What do you need from leadership in your organisation?
- How can leadership be a collective effort where a range of different people and styles contribute?

Challenge your everyday comments and beliefs about who and what behaviours are considered leader-like. Redesign systems and processes that reinforce the default model of leadership. Find, develop and showcase your existing and potential Quietly Powerful leaders.

Part IV contains further insights from the Quietly Powerful leader interviewees, their key attributes and how you can develop your Quietly Powerful leadership style.

Part IV

Quietly Powerful leadership

IF WE WANT more Quietly Powerful leaders in the world, we need individuals to step into Quietly Powerful leadership. Part IV is about what individuals can do to harness their quiet nature as leadership strengths. We also need organisations and leaders to find and develop the quiet talent, which will be explored in Part V.

Chapter 12

Quiet does not equal Quietly Powerful

Some of you may be thinking, 'But I know quiet leaders or quiet people who are not effective. They don't talk to people; they go off and do their own thing and we don't know what they're thinking most of the time.'

It's true, being quiet doesn't equal Quietly Powerful, it depends on what's driving the quiet behaviours. The following are some of these drivers which are quietly disempowering.

Ignorance and poor self-awareness

When I used to co-facilitate workshops with colleagues, I got some written feedback from a participant that threw me off guard. It said, 'Megumi was disengaged when she was not facilitating.'

I was horrified, as I was very passionate about these workshops and I thought I was giving my all to each and every one. Perhaps I was tired that day? Maybe I had a lapse in concentration?

But for someone to call me out as being disengaged, it could not have been just a momentary lapse.

What I came to realise, unfortunately, was that my focused listening face was misinterpreted as being disengaged. Partly due to my Japanese face and my introverted nature, my listening face can look blank and potentially as if I am thinking about something else. It is understandable that people would perceive me as being disengaged.

Since receiving this feedback and other similar feedback, I have learned to change my facial expressions more when listening. You will now see me nodding, smiling and vocalising 'hmm' or 'yes' more. I even practised using my eyebrows more because I heard that Japanese people don't tend to use their eyebrows much as part of their facial expression!

As a naturally quiet person, you may be misunderstood in a similar way. If you are not aware of how you are perceived, it can interfere with your communication and relationship building. It's worth finding out if this is the case and then you can make some small adjustments.

Caroline Stainkamph, Program Director at Vic ICT for Women, learned that she had to make an effort to vocalise her thoughts to avoid being misunderstood. She recalls:

> *What I came to realise was, if I sat there and said nothing because I was internally processing what I was thinking, then the other person was making assumptions about what [I was] thinking, and one of the assumptions was that she felt that I was opposing something she'd suggested, where, in actual fact, I wasn't. One of the things I've learned to do is say, 'Can I have a think about that, and I'll get back to you?'*

If you don't seek feedback and act on misperceptions, you can be quietly misunderstood.

Excuses, blaming and giving up too quickly

When I received the feedback about not appearing engaged, I went through a process of being upset and annoyed; I thought the participant was being harsh and making incorrect assumptions. My colleagues consoled me and told me that they didn't see me as disengaged and that the participant had simply misunderstood. At that point, I could have just said, 'Well, it's my style, my Japanese face and I can't do much about that!' and then done nothing about it.

However, in this instance, I cared enough about the impact I was having, so I didn't give up.

If you notice saying to yourself or to others: 'I can't do X, it's just not me' or 'I'm like this because I am X' you limit yourself by making excuses. If you say things like, 'I don't speak up because others won't listen' or 'people just don't understand me' then you limit yourself by blaming others or the system.

As described in Part II, there are many reasons for remaining quiet and hidden. It's useful to understand them, but you will remain quietly disempowered if you do nothing with the knowledge. It is a convenient way to stay inside your comfort zone.

> If you don't take responsibility to do something yourself, you will remain quietly limited.

Fear and anxiety

I remember the first culture workshop that I co-facilitated after my career change 18+ years ago. During the months of training in the lead-up to the workshop, I had been given countless feedback on what to do and say and what not to do and say. On the morning of the workshop, I got up early, meditated and reviewed my notes and rehearsed everything in my mind. When I arrived at the venue, my plan was to settle in and welcome the participants. While still nervous, I felt ready enough.

My experienced co-facilitator asked me to do a practice run of the section I would be facilitating. I obliged, though somewhat reluctantly, as I knew the participants would be arriving soon. As soon as I finished a couple of sentences, the experienced facilitator jumped in and told me to start again, saying that I needed to bring more energy into the room. A little shaken, I started again. After a short while, the facilitator stopped me and gave me another five pieces of feedback. I began to worry that I wasn't ready for the session. While I am sure the experienced facilitator was well-intentioned, it ended up being my worst experience of public speaking.

As I stood up to do my part of the workshop, I felt my voice shaking and I worried that I was visibly nervous. The session was fairly short and simple, so I managed to get through it, though on several occasions the experienced facilitator jumped in to re-explain what I had said. Fear and anxiety took over and there was no room for me to be present with the group or to use my quiet nature in a valuable way. I was quietly disempowered.

It's taken me a good decade to feel comfortable with presenting to and facilitating groups. It took a lot of repetition, feedback and meditation. Looking back, however, I could have sped up the learning process and built more confidence had I been encouraged to value and use my quieter approach.

Many people I coach share with me their anxiety about speaking up, being seen and being the centre of attention. The fear of being judged, being seen as incompetent or forgetting what to say and freezing are very common. From my experience, what makes it worse is the unrelenting inner critic that tells you off for every small thing you do wrong. Your attention is focused on the inner critic and not on the people you are speaking with.

> If you don't work with your inner critic, you will remain quietly absent.

Underestimating your impact

Many people I've met at public events or programs have said that they feel like there's no point in speaking up because they won't be listened to, or that others have already said what they'd been thinking and they have nothing else to add.

If you don't value your own contributions, you won't take active steps to get support or to find alternative ways to contribute.

> If you don't believe you can make an impact, or do little to enable yourself to make an impact, you will remain quietly disempowered.

If these drivers of quiet behaviour keep us disempowered, how is Quietly Powerful different?

Chapter 13

Three key attributes

If quiet does not equal Quietly Powerful, then what is Quietly Powerful? Three key attributes emerged as I interviewed Quietly Powerful leaders. They include being comfortable, being present and being purpose-driven:

1. **Being comfortable means:**
- Being authentic
- Acknowledging strengths and weaknesses
- Being comfortable sharing flaws, quirks or lack of knowledge
- Being humble and curious to learn
- Having self-compassion.

2. **Being present means being:**
- A great listener and observer
- Thoughtful
- Respectful and having meaningful relationships
- A great one-on-one mentor and coach
- Resilient and able to manage stress and anxiety.

3. **Being purposeful means being:**
- Focused on the work, the collective good and the right thing to do
- Inclusive and empowering
- Collaborative and not directive
- Able to share credit for achievements
- Able to build others up.

Being comfortable

Quietly Powerful leaders know themselves well and are comfortable with their strengths *and* weaknesses. They are transparent about their weaknesses and often surround themselves with people who are good at what they aren't. Humility comes naturally as a result. They have an inner confidence that allows them to say that they don't know everything and they can laugh at their weaknesses. Because these leaders are authentic and human, people around them feel more comfortable with them.

Dianne Jacobs, founding principal of The Talent Advisors and former partner at Goldman Sachs JBWere, is a quietly spoken person who struck me as being very comfortable in her own skin. I asked her what her secret was. Her view was that everyone brings strengths and unique perspectives, such that different people with different styles can achieve the same outcomes, but in different ways. By acknowledging this, you can become comfortable with your way of achieving outcomes. You can enjoy your strengths by knowing and using them effectively, while being careful not to overplay them.

Quietly Powerful leaders can be authentic, honest and show vulnerability.

Stacey Barr, who runs a successful training organisation around performance measurement and KPIs, finds it easy to admit when she doesn't know something. She said:

> *If you're asked a question [and] you're not sure of the answer to it, I found that if I just say, 'You know what? Off the top of my head, I don't know the answer to that, tell me a little bit more about it from your perspective...' It gives your brain a little bit of time to ponder and pull things together, and have a response. When you can be vulnerable in a group of people, they tend to have more trust in everything else you have to say.*

Clive Peter, mentioned in Chapter 2, makes a point of asking for feedback from his team, including calling out his own behaviours. He is keenly aware that he, like everyone, has blind spots and acknowledges the importance of having trusted people around him who feel safe enough to call him on them. He is also aware that it can be difficult for his team members to give him corrective feedback, so he works on establishing a norm of giving and receiving feedback with them. He would say:

> *You can always tell me what you think and if you think it's going to be a bit painful for me, close the door. I'll listen to it. I may not like it, but I'll listen to it. Because, I think, when you do that, you are able to learn.*

What goes hand in hand with this level of authenticity and openness to being vulnerable is humility. Quietly Powerful leaders, without exception, know that they don't know everything and they aren't overconfident as a result.

Steve Hodgkinson, CIO at the Victorian Department of Health and Human Services (DHHS), described how he adds value by knowing something, even if it's not everything.

> *It's a confidence you have that you can see things that not everybody can see. So, I think that's the starting point, because otherwise you don't feel you have anything to offer other than just going through process, which anyone can do. That doesn't mean that you're an expert or that you know everything, it just means that you see things that others may not.*

Three key attributes

The authenticity, vulnerability and humility based on being comfortable make these Quietly Powerful leaders human and approachable. The hallmark of their comfort within themselves was their self-deprecating humour. They had no problem pointing out some of their flaws or uniqueness as something to laugh about and they didn't take themselves too seriously.

Susan Allen, first mentioned in Chapter 1, had no problem sharing some of her 'quirky' side with her team. She never hid her fanatical support for Carlton Football Club, displaying a full-sized photograph of Chris Judd on the wall of her office. She also joked about how she wouldn't get off the dance floor at functions, which some would find surprising given how quietly spoken she is when you meet her.

Paul Boasman, mentioned in Chapters 1 and 4, told me that when he's stressed, he makes a beeline to his desk without seeing the people around him. He tells his team that he has such a tendency, so they know not to get concerned when he doesn't acknowledge them as he rushes past.

Yamini Naidu shared the story about the first time she told a joke about being Indian on stage. Owning her identity was a powerful step to demonstrate her comfort with herself and in being authentic. She was presenting to a large audience at IBM and noticed that the room was full of Indian engineers. She decided to have a go at sharing her Indian mother joke:

> *I said to my mum, 'I want to be a storyteller.' My mum replied, 'why can't you be a doctor or an IT professional?' And I did the whole Indian mother accent and the room just exploded with laughter. That was the first time that I had the courage to embrace my identity and also to just unleash my humour on stage.*

As an experienced speaker and storyteller, Yamini believes that what makes you different is the X-factor and that's what people want to see. It also shows that you are comfortable in your own skin. Yamini has now not only embraced her Indian identity, she has gone on to train in stand-up comedy!

Dr Jason Fox, mentioned in Chapter 2 and 3, unapologetically talks about his introversion in the first five minutes of his presentation. He jokes about how he would avoid the networking after the keynote presentations using a range of avoidance strategies like going to get a drink or going to the bathroom straight after a talk. By explaining his version of introversion, he clarifies that his introversion is not about being shy, but that his behaviours depend on the context and that he recharges his energy by being alone.

Every single Quietly Powerful leader I interviewed said that wholeheartedly being yourself is critically important and empowering. Being yourself doesn't mean you don't challenge yourself, learn new skills and try new things, it's about being true to yourself and being the best you can be.

Dr Jenny Brockis is a successful professional speaker on the topic of brain health. She is a quietly spoken medical doctor who used to enjoy one-on-one consultations as a practising GP. She now speaks to thousands of people and enjoys it; she feels that she can be herself on stage.

> *You don't have to pretend to be something you're not. I think the risk is we sometimes believe we have to behave in a certain way to fit in and meet the expectations of others. Knowing we have our own unique strengths and accepting we are enough, enables us to stay authentic, true to our own values and to be ourselves. There is nothing to be gained from being anyone but your true self, because this is what frees us up to play the bigger game. If we pretend, the only person being fooled is ourselves.*

Being comfortable with yourself is the pre-condition for authenticity, transparency and humility and gives you the courage to be vulnerable.

Being present

Quietly Powerful leaders have a powerful presence because they are present. They are mindful and not distracted, so they listen intently and speak only when necessary. They connect deeply, often one-to-one, and many have mentor and collegial relationships that have lasted for decades. They are present because they are comfortable within themselves, and they have learned to manage their anxieties and focus their attention on others.

Ruth Picker, partner at Ernst & Young, does a lot of listening by being fully present so she can listen beyond what people say. She said:

> *I don't only listen with my ears; I listen with my eyes and my heart. I look at people and I observe. How are they feeling? What's the mood in the room? How are they responding to what's being said? Are they engaged or disengaged? It's not only what they say, but it's what they don't say.*

This deep listening allows Ruth to check with people who have been quiet in a meeting to see whether they are okay. She makes a judgement call about whether to check during the meeting or afterwards and more often than not, the person who remained quiet has an issue or concern. Her listening ensures that people's concerns are heard and addressed.

Susan Allen explained that her listening and reflection were valuable leadership strengths for senior leaders. She used her presence to listen and learn from others to make informed and considered decisions. Not only that, people appreciated that Susan took others' ideas seriously and they felt encouraged to share again. She also listened and observed the leadership team dynamics in order to navigate through the politics of the workplace to get things done. She said:

> *I was on the leadership team of RACV as well as on the leadership team of VicRoads. You can sit back and read the politics to work*

out the motivations of the people around the room and how to help them achieve what they want to achieve rather than seeing it as a competition.

Similarly, after a few years in Ernst & Young's Australian practice after returning from Japan, Giovanni Stagno was pleasantly surprised to receive some feedback on his openness and willingness to listen. He said:

People felt very good about the fact that, regardless of organisation rank, I was genuine and authentic in listening and [I was] actually taking feedback or input onboard. It's easy to unconsciously dismiss someone's input when they are at a lower level within the organisation, as they usually don't have all the facts for any given circumstance. I was careful not to do that... people could say what they wanted to and knew they were heard.

Not only was listening important, he also made an effort to ensure that he was transparent, especially when difficult messages needed to be communicated. He shared his experience of when the business was not doing as well as expected; he communicated with his team early and transparently and he undertook steps to encourage working together in determining a positive way forward. This was a different approach to that of his peers who weren't prepared to communicate as openly about the uncertainty surrounding the business. While he felt vulnerable sharing the difficulties, he found that people appreciated his honesty as they could make their own informed decisions about what to do. He found that being present with his team was key to engaging and leading them on a change journey that other senior leaders were not ready to take.

Kevin Larkins, Interim CEO of The Bodhi Bus, spent many years working with Indigenous Australians. In his first role, he set up the first Alcohol and Drug Bureau in the Northern Territory. He realised at the time that in his 20 years of formal education he could only recall one talk on Indigenous Australians. The only

Three key attributes

Indigenous people he knew were footballers and boxers. He said that the most important learning he had was summed up by an Indigenous elder: 'If you want to know culture, come, sit down and listen. Don't talk, just listen.' This listening and openness to learn profoundly influenced his work with Indigenous people and their communities.

As you can see from the examples given by the Quietly Powerful leaders, a key leadership strength that many of them highlighted was effective listening – not just hearing the words but being present and considering what's been said and listening to what's not being said.

Another leadership strength listed by Quietly Powerful leaders is having strong one-on-one relationships. Brad Chan, first mentioned in Chapter 7, found that he enjoyed using his strengths in listening, analysis, inquiry and guiding to mentor and grow the people around him. He said:

> *I'm quite comfortable speaking in front of a large audience, but I think where I am most effective is using some of these natural gifts in [a] mentoring or coaching role. And I think a leader is also successful in relationships [because] you can get more meaningful relationships through those personal connections through engagement.*

Caroline Stainkamph also found that connecting with people helped her to bring the best out of her colleagues in order to develop high-performing teams.

> *I think what it's really helped me do is connect with my team. I really enjoy that one-on-one interaction and I think that's what can build [a] really strong relationship with your people. By getting to know your people, you start to understand their strengths and what their motivations are; you can help [and] shape the job that they're doing for you, so that you can make the most out of their skills and abilities.*

Similarly, Aneetha de Silva, Managing Director, Government at Aurecon, invests in building trusting one-on-one relationships. It enables effective group dynamics where people feel comfortable to contribute their views. She finds that reaching out to people on a personal level lets them know that she values their opinions. So often groups fall into groupthink or falling in line with the most senior person in the room. Aneetha invests in the one-to-one relationships so that she can tap into the collective wisdom to solve problems, generate new ideas and move forward *together*.

Your presence also impacts how you speak, not just how you listen.

A tip that Lisa Evans, mentioned in Chapters 1 and 6, shared was to 'be present rather than polished'. There are many tips on making yourself look more polished when public speaking, but if these tips get in the way of being authentic and present, it's not very helpful.

Ruth Picker described what she loves to do when public speaking:

> *I love to stand up on stage in front of a thousand people and deliver a public speech. Now, deliver a speech is probably not the right word because, I think why I'm a successful public speaker is because I treat the audience as a group of individuals [rather than as a group]. Sometimes I walk down onto the floor and engage with the audience as individuals, one by one. I love it. And I love asking them questions and getting feedback.*

Her approach to public speaking is to connect and engage, not to talk at people. It's a unique strength that allows her to build relationships on a large scale.

Our presence also has a significant impact on how effectively we navigate difficult conversations. Many of us find difficult conversations uncomfortable and our mental energy goes into preserving ourselves. We are more easily triggered and may say things in ways that can trigger the other person. When we're present, we can manage our thinking and emotional state to help the conversation. Clive Peter described how he has tough conversations respectfully and honestly:

> *Somebody once said to me that I had a conversation with him that was really difficult, but at the end of it, he didn't know whether he'd been hugged or pushed around. I try to have conversations that are honest and respectful, and I don't think that they need to be mutually exclusive no matter how tough the message is.*

He demonstrates honesty and respect by listening, playing back what he has heard and sharing his views clearly, explaining his logic and what is important and why. He is conscious of speaking in short sentences and speaks less so that the other person has opportunities to share their view. Clive doesn't shy away from acknowledging emotions either, as he believes that being authentic during difficult decisions and conversations is important.

Being present enables Quietly Powerful leaders to connect, build trust and understanding, listen deeply and have effective conversations.

Being purposeful

Quietly Powerful leaders are often reluctant leaders. They don't set out to gain power and control, and they prefer not to seek attention. When they do, it's for a purpose that they care about. The Quietly Powerful leaders step up because they want to make a difference and fulfil the organisation's mission; something bigger than themselves.

In my interview with Angie Paskevicius, CEO and Executive Director at Holyoake, I asked her about her career and she replied, 'I never really aspired to leadership or to become a CEO'. Her journey into leadership was driven by her desire to make a difference and be of service, which was instilled in her by her mother, who tirelessly volunteered to support people in fundraising. She also learned from her Lithuanian father – who came to Australia with nothing in his twenties – to persist in the face of adversity and strive to be the best that you can be.

She began her career as a speech pathologist because she wanted to help people with disabilities. She found herself leading speech pathology departments and then moving into general management roles. She then took an opportunity to lead a new start-up not-for-profit organisation and became the first CEO.

What keeps her grounded and committed to leadership in the not-for-profit sector includes her own experience of financial hardship, exposure to mental health issues, knowledge of homelessness, drug and alcohol issues and her earlier experiences of working with people with disabilities. Her empathy for people who find themselves in difficult life circumstances drives her willingness to lead. She described her leadership style in the context of having a clear purpose:

> *I'm a very calm leader. In fact, I'm an introvert. I know how to be an extrovert on the continuum. I can do all the things that I need to do as a CEO, but I do need time to recharge my batteries from time to time. I think what really drives my leadership style is that I'm very clear about who I am and what my purpose is and my 'why'. I'm very approachable, and I genuinely care about people. And I think that comes through in my leadership style.*

Steve Hodgkinson and his team at the Victorian DHHS have won many awards in recent years. What stands out is his ability to give credit to his team. An example of this is in one of his LinkedIn posts:

> *The Victorian DHHS is #2 in the Australian 2018 #CRIO50 Awards for ICT teams… cool! Up from #7 last year. This is all due to the excellent #DHHS technology leadership team: Fiona Sparks, Ray Baird, John Henderson, David Stephens, Liz Hughes also Marianne Walker and Jodie Quilliam and the many collaborative executives and staff across the department… and our*

partners Cenitex, Microsoft, Salesforce, CNI and many others. Thank you.

He then congratulated the other CIOs who were in the top 10. His focus is very much on the team and others, even though it was clearly an award for him, the CIO.

Steve also proudly told me that he successfully nominated two members of his leadership team for the Queen's Birthday Honours Public Service Medals – Jodie Quilliam in 2018 and Ray Baird in 2019 – unprecedented for technology roles in the public sector. He loves creating opportunities for his team to flourish and be recognised.

He is also a visible supporter of diversity and inclusion. After being named #2 in the CIO awards, he called out a lack of diversity; there was only one female CIO in the top 10 and nine in the top 50, saying, 'we all have more work to do.' His team also won the 2018 TechDiversity champion award for the RISE at DHHS program to create employment opportunities for people with autism. His sponsorship and support is making a difference.

Steve Hodgkinson extends his effort to inclusive activities, which involve actively communicating with people in the team. His team ran a branch meeting called 'You can't ask that!' where he and his directors agreed to answer anonymously submitted questions from staff. This was a powerful example of transparent communication and fearlessness to listen and be challenged, where the leaders ended up receiving positive feedback from staff.

The Quietly Powerful thought leaders and experts put themselves out in the public eye, even if they feel uncomfortable, because they want to help others with their message. Interestingly, many of these leaders now not only enjoy public speaking, they say they love it. Something seems to happen when our discomfort from being the centre of attention is overtaken by our passion to share our insights to help others.

Lisa Evans, who started her career as a neonatal intensive care specialist, overcame major challenges when she lost her hearing from a virus. In retraining her brain to hear in a different way, she became interested in public speaking, which led her to doing what she does now – empowering people to speak and tell their stories on stage. She said that she is still shy but she shines on stage because of the pleasure she gets from making a difference to people. She said:

> *I'm known as The Story Midwife, which is a tagline that one of my clients gave me. Even though I do love being on stage, what I love more than that is to empower others to step up and be on stage and to help them bring their stories into the world. It just gives me so much joy seeing others who may not have had the courage or skill to do so be able to step up and share their stories.*

When Dr Jenny Brockis decided to share her thought leadership on brain health, she left her general medical practice where she felt comfortable building safety and trust in her one-on-one or small group consultations. Her mission to help people with their brain health meant that she had to speak to large groups and learn new ways to engage and be heard. She said:

> *This was such a steep learning curve, but because I passionately believed the messages I had to share were important, I knew I had to move from speaking one-to-one to many. As scary as that was for a natural introvert, by staying true to my message and understanding this [wasn't] about me and all about helping others to achieve greater success and happiness, this made the prospect of stepping onto a stage slightly less terrifying.*

When you are purpose-driven, it allows you to persist in the face of difficulties and to do things that may be outside your comfort zone. It's a powerful trait of any leader and is one that shines brightly in Quietly Powerful leaders.

~

Three key attributes

The three key attributes of Quietly Powerful leaders are mutually reinforcing. Being comfortable in ourselves allows us to be more present with others, as we worry less about ourselves. Being present allows us to serve a purpose, to focus on others, the work, the team or the cause. Being purposeful allows us to stretch ourselves, potentially gain additional skills and behaviours and still be comfortable with who we are.

Mutually reinforcing attributes of Quietly Powerful leaders

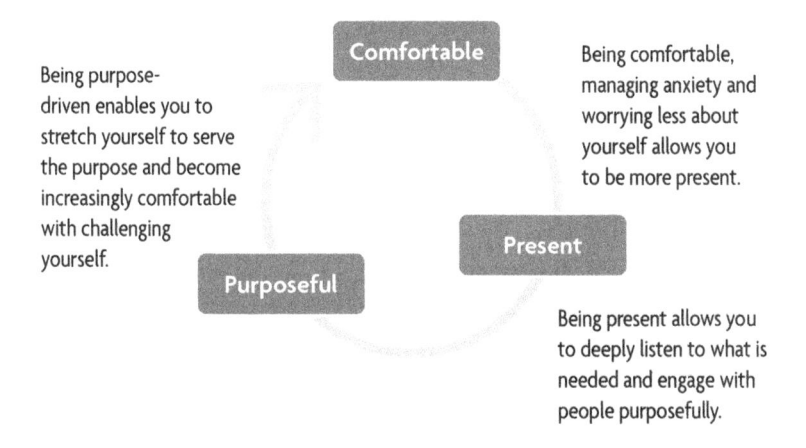

Comfortable

Being comfortable, managing anxiety and worrying less about yourself allows you to be more present.

Present

Being present allows you to deeply listen to what is needed and engage with people purposefully.

Purposeful

Being purpose-driven enables you to stretch yourself to serve the purpose and become increasingly comfortable with challenging yourself.

What makes these leaders powerful?

- **They step into leadership roles for a bigger purpose than themselves.** They wouldn't have done so unless there was a compelling reason for them to step up. Their interest in the collective – the team, organisation or purpose – is stronger than their self-interest. They tend to demonstrate servant leadership as a result.

- **They don't develop a sense of entitlement or self-importance;** they remain humble and aren't 'poisoned' by power – thinking that they are better than others. They haven't lost empathy for others; they have an ability to listen and show respect to everyone regardless of rank and position. Humble leadership comes naturally to them.

- **They develop their own style of leadership.** As they don't step into leadership roles to impress or to gain power for power's sake, it's important for them to feel authentic. They work on identifying and nurturing their own style of leadership.
- **They're committed to their own development.** Sometimes they are reluctant leaders because they know that they're missing some skills, such as public speaking. Because they're aware of this, they're committed to developing these skills and often excel in them after practice.
- **They look for opportunities to develop others,** as they know how much they've benefited from having mentors and supporters. Some have kept in touch with mentees for decades. They support and develop others not out of a sense of obligation but out of the joy of seeing others succeed. They tend to be development-focused leaders.
- **They are inclusive and lift others up.** They promote their team's work, the organisation and people they serve more than themselves. They are truly inclusive because they involve a variety of people who can contribute to the work, regardless of seniority, background or style.

Chapter 14

Quiet superpowers

When leaders have developed a sense of comfort with themselves and are present and purposeful, they're no longer quietly disempowered and they can use their quiet superpowers to:

- **Access calm.** Some quiet people can be perceived as calm, even if they're stressing out inside. When you use strategies to calm your nervous system, people will not only perceive you as calm, but they will be calmed by your presence.
- **Be aware and reflective.** When you create space for calm and quiet, you can reflect and deepen your awareness about yourself and your impact. You can be open to feedback while discerning what's helpful. Rather than just moving from task to task, reflective space enables you to learn and grow. You have greater access to a better version of yourself.
- **Listen, observe and sense.** By being quiet and present you can pick up so much of what is happening in a team, a conversation, a meeting, coaching, negotiations and even when you're presenting. By being present with others, your attention is on them and the conversation, not on yourself

or your thoughts. It allows for deep listening and being perceptive in your observations and sensing.

- **Connect and create.** Deep listening and reflection enables you to connect and make sense of ideas that others may not. Making sense of disparate ideas is one powerful approach to creativity. Noticing contradictions is another pathway to insight. While groups can spark ideas, individual reflection is essential to creative thinking.

- **Be humble and curious.** 'Humility is not thinking less of yourself, it's thinking of yourself less,' said British author, C.S. Lewis. By thinking of yourself less and valuing others, you relate to people with respect. You also acknowledge that you don't have all the answers, so you naturally become curious, inquisitive and inclusive.

- **Ask wise questions.** Wise questions only emerge through great listening and curiosity. Having heard and noticed more than others, you can ask questions that no one else is asking, you can generate insight through deeper questions and build understanding.

- **Use silence comfortably.** Silence creates space for deep thinking. When you are comfortable and present, you can be in silence without feeling like you have to fill the void. When you are comfortable with the silence, it allows others to be comfortable with it as well. Silence is golden in solitude and when interacting with others – such as in coaching – through difficult conversations and public speaking.

- **Build deeper relationships.** You may not have the gift of the gab to entertain, but your presence, listening and questions allow you to make deeper connections. People feel safe, listened to and valued when they are with you.

- **Grow safety and trust.** People know that you will listen and take them seriously. They feel safe to speak openly with you, including giving you constructive feedback. People don't feel they need to hide anything, so the bad news is shared as much as the good. Trust is built both ways.

- **Coach with impact.** Powerful coaching happens when the person being coached does most of the thinking and talking. A quiet approach and being prompted by wise questions allows space for people to think. The quiet strengths of listening, focusing on the other person, trust and deep one-on-one relationships are big advantages when coaching.

- **Hold difficult conversations respectfully.** The quiet approach to difficult conversation involves listening to understand. When done well, differences are addressed before they turn into conflict. Difficult conversations are approached with patience and an intention to work with the other person to address differences. Silence is critical during difficult conversations, as Susan Scott, author of *Fierce Conversations*, says: 'let silence do the heavy lifting.'

- **Share and empower.** Truly empowering people requires you to step back and create the space for people to step in. You can only share power by being comfortable with your own worth and contribution. You don't need the spotlight; you take pride in shining the spotlight on someone else. When you do, capable people will surprise themselves with what they never thought was possible.

- **Influence through understanding.** The quieter approach to influencing is one of individual consultation and inclusion. It involves speaking with key stakeholders one-on-one to hear their concerns and work through them to get to a solution. They tend not to push their ideas through with persuasive talk in groups. Good negotiators use silence rather than filling in the space.

- **Sell by helping, not pushing.** There is often an assumption that quieter people cannot sell. The quieter approach to selling involves more listening and less pushy selling. It is less about self-promotion and more about helping people with what they are buying, whether it's a product, service or a cause. Introverts do better at sales by focusing on transparent, authentic and low-pressure selling, according to Matthew Pollard, author of *The Introvert's Edge*.

- **Solve complex problems without rushing.** A quieter, reflective approach means you don't rush decisions. While it may feel slow for some people, it is how organisations can avoid over-simplifying complex problems or covering them up with quick fixes. It is also a way to minimise biased, under-informed decisions coloured by our cognitive biases.

- **Focus on the audience when speaking.** Many people shy from public speaking as they dislike being the centre of attention. Focusing on the audience then becomes a strength. A quiet approach to public speaking involves solid preparation and involving the audience. Public speaking is a skill that can be learned, and many great speakers are naturally quiet. Great storytellers and public speakers also pause, slow down and gain greater attention.

- **Include everyone in group discussions.** The tendency to focus on the other person translates to facilitating group discussions without over-involvement. This is demonstrated by listening, connecting ideas and the ability to draw ideas out of the group. If you want the group to do the work successfully, get a skilled facilitator who can use their quiet strength.

Great care, depth and wisdom come from quiet approaches. Most people would willingly contribute their best when treated this way. Wouldn't it be helpful to access half or even just a few of these superpowers as a leader? Imagine how many more people will get on board with your mission or purpose and how much more you can achieve together.

> **Ruth Picker's Leadership Principles**
>
> Ruth shared her leadership principles in our interview, which relates closely to the quiet superpowers. She actively applies these principles to her everyday leadership. The acronym CALMER stands for:
>
> > Care
> > Authentic
> > Listen
> > Mentor/Motivate
> > Empower
> > Respect

Chapter 15

The path to Quietly Powerful

The key attributes of Quietly Powerful leaders provide a guide for how you might move from feeling quietly disempowered to feeling powerful. In this chapter, I invite you to get a sense of where you are now on the path to feeling Quietly Powerful. Then I will provide some direction for how you might develop yourself.

Where are you now?

Here are some statements to see where you are on the journey to becoming Quietly Powerful. How strongly would you agree with these statements? The results will allow you to see where you might focus your efforts in developing yourself.

Quietly Powerful self-assessment

Comfortable:
- I feel comfortable with my strengths and can easily and clearly describe them.
- I am accepting of my weaknesses and am comfortable to share them with others.
- I feel comfortable sharing stories about myself with others.
- I feel comfortable being myself and I don't feel the need to fit in.
- I don't feel like I have to hide my true self.
- I have compassion for myself and am not overly critical when I make a mistake or don't achieve a goal.
- I have supportive, positive inner voices which can minimise the chances of negative, critical voices overpowering me.

```
1    2    3    4    5    6    7    8    9    10
|____|____|____|____|____|____|____|____|____|
Strongly disagree                    Strongly agree
```

Present:
- I am effective at managing my anxiety and fears. For example, I have strategies to manage my emotions when I'm asked to do a presentation or when I'm put on the spot.
- I can manage my mental and emotional state so that people experience me as being fully present with them.
- I am an effective listener, even when under pressure.
- People often feel a calming presence from me, even when I'm under stress or pressure.
- My presence helps me to connect with people.
- I can catch myself when I'm distracted by my own thoughts or outside distractions.
- I can easily come back to the present moment when I notice I've wandered off.

```
1    2    3    4    5    6    7    8    9    10
|____|____|____|____|____|____|____|____|____|
Strongly disagree                    Strongly agree
```

Purposeful:
- I feel purposeful about the things I do.
- I often think about the bigger purpose of what I'm doing.
- I feel passionate about the things I'm trying to achieve.
- I'm clear about my values and feel I live by and demonstrate them in what I do.
- I have a strong sense of personal mission or life purpose.
- My purpose and mission pull me to do things I wouldn't normally do or at times things I feel are outside my comfort zone.
- My purpose and mission enable me to be persistent, even in the face of obstacles.

1	2	3	4	5	6	7	8	9	10

Strongly disagreeStrongly agree

Development from the inside out

The challenge with the Quietly Powerful leader attributes is that you don't become more comfortable, present and purposeful by someone telling you to be these things or by learning a few skills.

Imagine if I told you to be more comfortable with your weaknesses. I imagine your brain would go crazy with thoughts such as, 'But I don't like my weaknesses', 'How can I be comfortable with them when I keep getting feedback to fix them?' or 'But I am *so* bad at X.'

You need an inside-out development process that allows you to actually *feel* comfortable, present and purposeful.

Unfortunately, it's the outside-in approaches that quiet professionals are told they need to adopt. Training on presentation and assertiveness skills, body language, image, appearance and personal branding many leave you feeling disempowered because it's not built on a solid foundation of inner quiet power. It feels more like you're having to fake it. If you tend to compare yourself with others, you risk feeling worse when you see others in the training doing the techniques better. These feelings add to your critical inner voices, amplifying the internalised marginalisation described in Chapter 7.

When I was learning to facilitate the leadership and culture workshops, my colleagues and I had to facilitate a part of the workshop in front of each other and the teachers and receive feedback. As a quiet-natured facilitator, I was regularly told to 'bring more energy'. The more I was told that, the more I felt anxious that I would never be able to do what my colleagues were doing. The more anxious I got, the more my energy shrank in the room. It was a vicious cycle. One day I decided to go all out and be energetic and bubbly. Sadly, the feedback I received was 'Good try, but you're not being yourself.' I was really lost as to what to do from there.

It took me many years to recover from the confusing feedback and work out what I needed to do. It really was about becoming comfortable with myself and shifting the attention away from my inner critic. This allowed me to be present. I already had a strong passion for making a positive difference to the people I was with, I just needed to work on my inner beliefs, thoughts and feelings.

All the skills training that focuses on techniques and tools is important but it's not enough, especially if you're having to deal with strong inner critics and past conditioning that has caused you to disregard yourself in some way. Connecting with and valuing your real self is a critical step that's missed too often.

Fitting in and following the formula robs you of bringing your whole self to a situation.

Yamini Naidu told me that embracing her unique identity gave her a step up in the impact she had in her professional speaking. She believes that people are moving away from the formulaic approach as well. She said:

> *In the '90s, and even in the 2000s, people would go by the presentation skills program, which were very cookie cutter.*

They would say, 'Stand here! Look there! Raise your hand!' And now people just don't buy that.

Similarly, Dr Jason Fox, who amplifies the quirky side of his introversion and professorship, also had to unlearn techniques to embrace a more authentic approach to speaking. He recalled:

Learning the ropes of professional speaking and then actually stepping into my own style meant unlearning a lot of stuff. We are taught to be confident and certain, but sometimes this means people don't question their own assumptions. It all feels contrived to me – like a platitude without depth of meaning.

With so many messages about how you should behave to be leader-like, your authentic identity can get lost. People don't warm to a polished leader and they don't connect with someone who is always 'professional'.

If you want to be an authentic leader, you have to find and re-engage with yourself, and go beyond just looking the part.

Don't wait for the system to change

For quiet professionals, it can be frustrating being overlooked because of style and exhausting trying to fit in by being more vocal and looking the part. It would be wonderful if organisations and society valued the quality of quiet more than they do now. It would certainly make it easier for quiet professionals to be noticed for their talents and for them to achieve greater success.

You could be waiting for a long time though. As much as we'd like others to change and see our point of view, it will take time and effort for people to see things differently. As with many diversity and inclusion initiatives, change in people's beliefs and perceptions takes a while. So, don't wait for others and the system to change. You can start on your inside-out development regardless of how quickly the system changes. It's an opportunity to be the best you can be in your own unique way and, by doing so, people will start to feel your presence and impact.

Let's get into the strategies for how you, as an individual, can start feeling more powerful without feeling like you have to fake it.

The two-part strategy to Quietly Powerful

A coaching client – let's call her Jane – called me to find out about Quietly Powerful leadership. Jane had attended one of the Quietly Powerful breakfasts, read some articles and felt that her efforts to overcome her weaknesses over the years through professional development had not worked for her. When she called me, the first thing she said was, 'Megumi, I really need help. I have so many things I have to fix, I've done all this training and there's still so much to do.'

I listened to her as she described the training she had done and why she felt she wasn't developing as she had expected to. I then said to her, 'Jane, I have a feeling that one of the first things we need to fix is your feeling that you have to 'fix' yourself.'

There is a better, two-part strategy:

1. Appreciate fully: Work on appreciating your natural qualities and expanding your skillsets; and

2. Adapt purposefully: Adapt and add your natural skills for a purpose instead of trying to replace what you have.

Appreciate fully

Appreciating fully is about valuing *all* of yourself, not just the parts you like about yourself. Some of the strength-based approaches to coaching tend to focus on the parts you like. While the positivity of the strength-based approaches is valuable, it's incomplete. You are only appreciating yourself partially and risk neglecting the parts of yourself you don't like or consider to be weaknesses.

Everything may be fine on the surface, but you may be left with a subconscious sense of shame or disappointment with yourself around these weaknesses.

If you felt unsure or rated yourself lower on the 'Comfortable' and 'Present' questions in the Quietly Powerful Self-Assessment, I suggest you take a look at how much you appreciate yourself fully.

It's very difficult to be comfortable with yourself if you haven't done the work to understand and accept who you are and why you are the way you are. Without that sense of comfort, you are more easily distracted by self-critical and self-limiting thoughts and you can't be present when you need to be. It's also difficult to find a mission and purpose without a sense of who you are and who you could become. You need a strong foundation of knowing and valuing yourself.

Adapt purposefully

Adapting purposefully is different to fixing yourself, in that you have a compelling reason for adapting yourself. You are tapping into the 'Free Trait Theory' mentioned in Chapter 4, where you can behave out of character or do things you never thought you could when you have a strong enough purpose that pulls you. Fixing yourself, on the other hand, lives in the world of 'shoulds'. You tell yourself that you *should* behave in certain ways to fit in, to be seen as leader-like and to be recognised.

If you felt unsure or rated yourself lower on the 'Present' and 'Purposeful' questions in the Quietly Powerful Self-Assessment, I suggest you take a look at whether you are adapting yourself purposefully.

The energy with which you learn new skills and behaviours, the persistence with which you practise and the enjoyment you get from achieving something you never thought you could, are completely different to adapting purposefully and fixing yourself. In addition, when you adapt purposefully, you build on the valuable qualities and skills you already have, rather than replacing them. You are simply growing your repertoire of ways of being.

The key is to develop the precious qualities which you or others may deem not valuable, rather than replace or marginalise them. It's this combination of predispositions and the additional qualities and skills that enables you to be authentically Quietly Powerful.

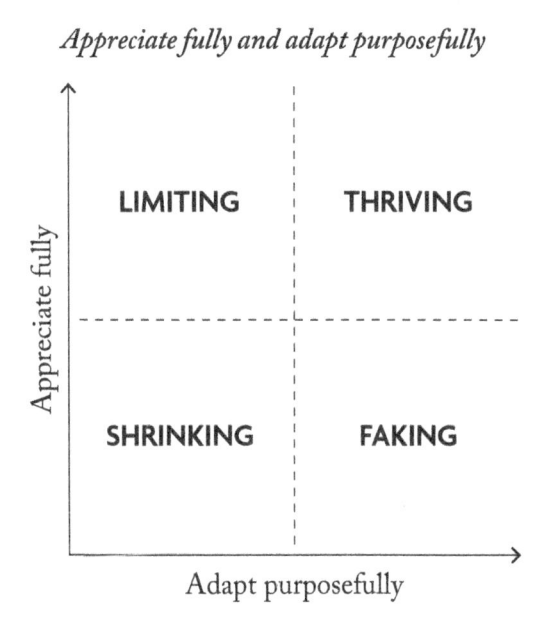

Appreciate fully and adapt purposefully

	Adapt purposefully →	
Appreciate fully ↑	LIMITING	THRIVING
	SHRINKING	FAKING

You need to work on both parts to feel powerful within yourself while remaining authentic. Like Jane, many people have told me that they have worked on one part and not the other, which still leaves them feeling disempowered. Let's look at why both parts are necessary.

Shrinking: Not appreciating or adapting

You'll shrink if you don't appreciate yourself fully or adapt purposefully. You'll feel disempowered and inadequate and be too afraid to make any changes. You'll hold yourself back from taking up opportunities. Do you find yourself hiding whenever you can? Are you afraid of trying or learning anything new? When you don't challenge yourself, your self-esteem is negatively affected over time. In other words, you shrink.

You're stuck in the shrinking box if you hear yourself saying:

- 'I've never been good at…'
- 'I wish I was more like…'
- 'I'm happy to be in the background…'
- 'It's just how I am…'
- 'I couldn't possibly…'

Talented professionals stay small and remain in the background because they put themselves down and remain in their comfort zones. Talent is wasted and opportunities are missed. People in this shrinking place have been conditioned to be blind to their potential. Throughout their lives, they may have been told to be happy with what they already have and not to ask for more.

Limiting: Appreciating but not adapting

Some of you may have decided to stick with the cards that you were dealt; you appreciate yourself fully and see no point or make any effort in adapting yourself. You've made peace with who you are and worry less about what others think of you. You become comfortable with saying no to opportunities that don't fit with your strengths. You may even tell your managers upfront about how to get the best out of you, based on a solid understanding of your natural tendencies.

This level of awareness and acceptance of your predispositions is healthy and empowering. Where it becomes limiting is when you use them as excuses such as:

- 'I'd rather focus on using my strengths.'
- 'That's just not me. I'm sticking with what I'm good at and what I know.'
- 'I'm not the networking type.'
- 'I'm happy with how I am. I don't want people trying to change me.'
- 'I'm just being myself.'

When we say things like this, we create an imaginary box that defines who we think we are, and we get stuck inside it. We then miss out on the opportunity to grow and expand our repertoire, and we limit ourselves to our comfort zones.

There is a number of reasons you might limit yourself in your imaginary comfortable box. It could be that you had a frightening experience doing something outside of your comfort zone, where you may have been humiliated or felt an intense sense of failure and shame. You may have been warned by others not to take risks and internalised that message. It could be that you don't feel a strong enough sense of purpose to pull you out of the box. People who challenge themselves typically have a strong achievement orientation, competitiveness or a sense of purpose that is bigger than themselves.

Human beings are capable of growing and evolving, as shown by studies into neuroplasticity. Whether it's something you're good at or not yet good at, you can always get better with effort. This is the growth mindset that Dr Carol Dweck, author of *Mindset: The New Psychology of Success*, speaks and writes about. It's a critical mindset required for success and fulfilment in life. With a fixed mindset, you stay inside your imaginary box and you can't live your life to the fullest.

Faking: Adapting but not appreciating

Some of you courageously challenge yourselves by regularly stepping outside of your comfort zones. You invest in your personal and professional development. You read books and seek feedback and coaching from colleagues and coaches. You are constantly looking for ways to improve yourself. While that is admirable and courageous, you could hit a brick wall if you only focus on improving yourself. It may start to feel like you'll never be good enough or as if you're having to put on the fake persona to apply the techniques and skills you've learned.

Unfortunately, these feelings intensify when well-intentioned colleagues, teachers and coaches try to replace some of our 'weaknesses' with skills and behaviours demonstrated by people who are perceived to be successful. This is especially common in the business world, where people are skewed towards masculine and extroverted behaviours, such as being assertive, speaking up, looking confident, being decisive, networking effectively and speaking persuasively.

While these skills and behaviours are indeed necessary to succeed in masculine and extrovert preferred environments, you risk devaluing the precious qualities that are natural to you if you try to adopt them. When you constantly put on a brave face and behave this way, it can come across as fake or 'trying too hard'. Worse, people won't connect with the real you and you will start to lose your sense of self. You are essentially 'covering' your real self and it can lead to exhaustion and burnout.

Some of us have mastered these skills and behaviours, to the extent that people perceive our fake personas to be real. If we deeply listen to ourselves, though, we know we're faking it and we can feel hollow.

Thriving: Appreciating fully *and* adapting purposefully

As I have said, you can thrive by appreciating what you have and building on it. When you have a good understanding and appreciation of your natural qualities, you have a better foundation on which to grow and evolve. Those learned skills and behaviours will integrate rather than replace or marginalise your natural qualities.

It's like building the foundations of a house. With a solid foundation, you can build different types of houses and even add extensions. Without a solid foundation, you're limited in what you can build or you can end up with an unstable house.

With an appreciation of your natural qualities, you can harness their power and build on them such that you thrive on both the natural and learned abilities. You can be comfortable with what you see as your weaknesses and harness the positive essence in them as well.

The learning process becomes more enjoyable, as it's an addition and integration exercise. You become braver at experimenting and learning new skills because you know you can fall back on what you have already. The more you challenge yourself, face difficulties, achieve goals or simply make progress, the more you feel you can handle difficulties and setbacks.

The process of appreciating and harnessing your natural qualities, as well as growing and developing, is ongoing. This dual process strengthens you and the two forces start to feel complementary. The more you learn, the more you appreciate what you have. The more you appreciate what you have, the more you're able to stretch yourself. You thrive and become Quietly Powerful.

Susan Allen told me that she was able to progress in her career because she had managers who would give her opportunities that were outside her comfort zone. What gave her the courage to have a go was that her managers believed in her abilities and that she could do more. Her confidence grew from taking on these challenges. She said:

> *You know, women in particular suffer from impostor syndrome, often saying, 'I couldn't possibly do that, I'm not qualified for that.' I think it's really important to aim at something when you're 80 per cent there. Take the opportunity to grab a position that will enable you to learn and develop [and] try and develop your own leadership style. Don't try to imitate someone else, otherwise you will come across as inauthentic.*

It takes courage, not confidence, to take on these challenges. Confidence comes later. And courage grows from connecting with who we are and who we could be to serve our purpose. Brené Brown, first mentioned in Chapter 8, highlights the importance of courage. Her message is to: 'Choose courage over comfort. Choose whole hearts over armour. And choose the great adventure of being brave and afraid. At the exact same time.'

Living fully in this way requires being okay with failure, criticism and setbacks. This requires being comfortable with yourself and feeling a sense that you're okay, regardless of what's happening on the outside, what others say or whether you meet others' expectations. Appreciating yourself fully helps you to be brave and do what needs to be done in the service of your mission and purpose.

You can now see how appreciating fully and adapting purposefully moves you towards feeling Quietly Powerful. Let's next look at the practical steps to take to appreciate yourself fully and to adapt purposefully in Chapters 16 and 17.

Chapter 16

Appreciate fully

I realise that if I were to tell you to appreciate yourself fully, it wouldn't be much different to people advising you to 'be more confident', 'believe in yourself' and 'back yourself'.

In this chapter, I will share the steps, practical tips and lessons from the Quietly Powerful leader interviewees and my own experiences. While it's impossible to detail everything involved, I am introducing a few techniques and skills involved to get you started in appreciating yourself fully.

In a nutshell, appreciating fully involves three major steps:

1. Understanding yourself and the story you tell yourself.
2. Reframing and shaking up your beliefs about yourself.
3. Leveraging your uniqueness strategically.

Three steps to appreciating fully

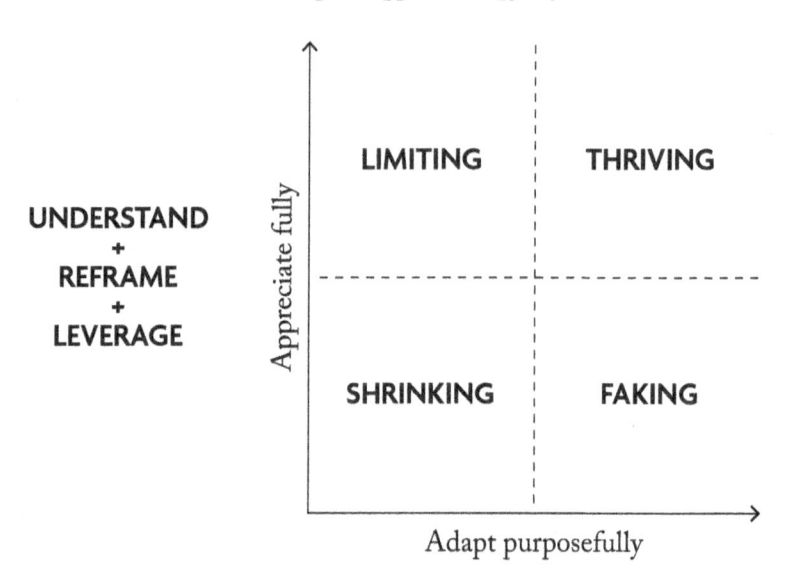

```
                        ↑
                        |
               LIMITING | THRIVING
                        |
UNDERSTAND          ┌   |
    +               │   |
  REFRAME       fully── — — — — — — — — — →
    +           Appreciate|
 LEVERAGE           └   |
                        |
              SHRINKING | FAKING
                        |
                        └─────────────────→
                        Adapt purposefully
```

1. Understand yourself and the story you tell yourself

The first thing to do to appreciate yourself fully is to learn more about yourself. I used to think I knew myself well when I was in my twenties until I was introduced to a range of self-awareness raising tools and techniques. I was shocked at how little I knew about myself. The more I've learned about myself, the more I feel there is to learn. What are more interesting to me these days are the stories I tell myself about my predispositions and why I am the way I am. They are literally stories I've made up in my head. What I notice about them is that they have a lot to do with how I'm able to do some things and not others.

One of the long-standing stories I'd told myself was that because English was my second language until I was about twenty, my vocabulary was quite limited and I would never be able to do work or activities that required a lot of writing. I still do have that thought sometimes – especially as I write books! I have this little voice that says: 'What on earth are you doing writing books? You've never been a great writer; you have to use the thesaurus all the time.'

So, the story I tell myself goes: 'English was my second language, I missed some important years of school in Australia, my vocabulary is limited, my grammar is mixed up sometimes, so I don't write well.' But the story I've been trying to adopt, with some help from friends, colleagues and positive feedback from readers, is: 'Because English was my second language I don't use complicated words and I've learned to structure my thinking and writing so that it's clear and simple for people to understand'.

It doesn't matter how true these stories are. The latter story allows me to have a go at writing and by having a go over and over again I'm getting better. The former story nearly stopped me from posting my first blog in 2015. Since then I have written more than 90 articles, a self-published book and this book. *The story you tell yourself matters.*

To understand yourself and the stories you tell yourself, I invite you to go on an exploration of your natural qualities, inner voices, conditioning and your resulting beliefs.

Understand your natural qualities

To understand your natural qualities, use a range of profiling tools, coaches, mentors and people you trust who can give you honest feedback.

Pick profiling tools which measure your natural tendencies, rather than behaviours you have adopted, to be effective in the workplace or tools which measure helpful versus unhelpful behaviours. What you want to understand is what comes most naturally to you. When you know that, you can start to look for what you can do to make the most of what you have. For most of us, it is not sustainable to go against our nature all the time.

Ask people who have known you for a long time, as well as people who have only known you for a short time. It's useful to know the similarities and differences between someone's early impression and how they see you when they get to know you.

Notice your reaction when you uncover your natural qualities. You could be very pleased to have some of them and perhaps not others. For example, you may be very proud that you're a people person. On the other hand, you may be frustrated with how you don't stand your ground when pushed by people who are dominating. Your reaction will give you an insight into the story you tell yourself.

Understand your inner voices and their impact

The stories we tell ourselves show up in sneaky ways through our inner voices. Some of these voices are loud and constant and others pop up occasionally when we're about to do something, especially when trying something new or daring.

Most of us have a mix of positive, neutral and negative voices. They may be about ourselves, other people or situations that we're in.

Positive voices might be helpful and supportive like, 'Just have a go, what's the worst that could happen?' or, 'You've been through much tougher times than this, you can manage.' Neutral voices might be observations such as, 'You're starting to get agitated by Bob.' Negative voices are those that are critical, such as 'Why do you keep getting nervous when you speak?' or voices that hold you back like, 'Don't show off, you'll be seen as a brag and people won't like you.'

These inner voices might be about other people, too. A helpful one might be a voice like, 'Something must have happened for her to not call today.' While a neutral one would be, 'She didn't call.' And a negative one would be, 'How dare she not call today!'

Most of the time we don't pay attention to these voices, as they run in the background and aren't loud enough to hear in our busy

Appreciate fully

lives. If you do some quiet activities like yoga or meditation, you might find that these voices get louder and clearer. Sometimes they become so loud that they stop us from falling asleep or they wake us up in the middle of the night.

Regardless of whether you hear them or not, they still drive your behaviours. Without examining these inner voices, you'll end up being stuck with them. The neuropathways for these voices have been well-established and they become your go-to pathway.

Take a look at the contrasting voices below, they are common inner voices that run in our heads when we're in a group meeting. Which ones do you hear more often?

Negative	Neutral	Positive
'Everyone else in the room is so much smarter than me.'	'Everyone in the room has some expertise required for this meeting.'	'Everyone, including me, has something to contribute to this meeting.'
'They don't know what they're talking about.'	'I can't make sense of what they're talking about.'	'There's something they know that I don't know, and possibly something I know that they don't know.'
'See, no one is going to listen to me anyway.'	'Looks like they didn't really hear me this time.'	'I wonder if there's something in the way of them hearing me?'

I know my default voices used to be like those in the left-hand column. In fact, I know these voices slip back sometimes, because they've been my default for a long time. It can take a lot of effort to catch and challenge these voices.

Your inner voices – the ones you listen to – drive your response to situations and other people. Depending on which of the above voices you decide to adopt, can you see how you might behave differently in a meeting?

As part of understanding yourself and the story you tell yourself, you need to keep track of these inner voices as they will offer hints about your story.

Explore how you've been conditioned

These inner voices go hand in hand with your conditioning. You might even be able to work out the exact person who used to say these things to you. For example, you may have been blessed to have had a sports coach who encouraged you to have a go, even if you hadn't done something before, or you may have had a teacher who told you to stop fiddling when you spoke because it made you look nervous, or maybe a parent told you not to get a big head when you told them about the good score you got on a test.

As explored in Chapters 4 to 7, we hear and interpret all kinds of messages about who we are, how we should be, what is valued and what is not. It may have been because of our personalities or our cultural, social or religious upbringing or if we felt we were in the mainstream or minority. Our current thoughts could be a product of all these messages we've absorbed until now.

The story you tell yourself is a story you've unconsciously made up from various experiences and other people's opinions.

We see things not as they are, but as we are.
—H.M. Tomlinson

By exploring your conditioning, you'll understand why you do what you do. Once you know this, you'll be ready to challenge and reframe your thinking and beliefs so that they work for you rather than against you.

2. Reframe and shake up your beliefs

Once you've explored your natural qualities, inner voices and conditioning, it's time to check and challenge the stories you tell yourself about them. You can put yourself in a box, decide that you're a certain way and that's just who you are. But it's a guaranteed way of limiting yourself and staying small. In a rigid box, there's no room for growth.

Neuroscientists now support the concept of neuroplasticity – that is, the plasticity or malleability of the brain. With practice and repetition, our brains and abilities can change, not just for physical activities but also for thoughts and beliefs. Reframing allows you to choose a more flexible box, which can give you the opportunity to expand yourself by growing into who you *could* become.

After exploring your qualities and the stories you tell yourself, here are two exercises:

1. Reframe your strengths and weaknesses.

2. Negotiate with your negative inner voices.

Reframe your strengths and weaknesses

Listen to the story you tell yourself. You make judgements about your qualities being either strengths or weaknesses. For example, quiet people may label their quiet nature as a weakness or disadvantage. Not many people would pick their quiet nature as a strength. Some would instead choose qualities like being structured and organised as a strength.

Firstly, take a weakness and see how it could be reframed as neutral, or even as a strength, by finding the essence of the quality that is useful. If you're quiet, this isn't necessarily good or bad. Using your quietness well, you could be the one who listens and people may come to you because you're a good listener. You could be the one who brings calm in a chaotic environment, one with a quiet determination or one who allows your team to shine. Weaknesses reframed can become a strength.

There are many qualities you can reframe in this way. For example, my limited vocabulary can be used to write simply, my agreeableness can be used well to manage difficult relationships and slow thinking can be helpful for deep and thorough problem-solving. As you keep reframing them, you'll start to realise that most qualities can be both strengths and weaknesses. When you look at your qualities in that way, it's harder to feel ashamed about your weaknesses, isn't it? It gives you a larger repertoire of strengths to draw on. Some of these reframed weaknesses can become differentiators, too.

What we see as strengths and weaknesses, positive or negative, good or bad, all depend on your perspective.

Secondly, take a strength and identify when that quality is useful and when it could become a weakness, especially when overused or relied too much on. With the example of being structured and organised, it can be a great strength to use in managing a lot of activities and people, ensuring details aren't overlooked and results are achieved in a disciplined manner. But on the flipside, if you rely too much on structure and discipline, you might miss indicators when plans need to change, you might not be open to radical ideas that could achieve the same, or better, results or you could be perceived as overly process-reliant, risk averse or rigid.

What you perceive as strengths may not always be useful, depending on the situation and how you use your strengths.

Appreciate fully

Appreciating and harnessing your strengths is a rewarding strategy that successful people have used in many fields. The key is to be aware of overuse, misuse or over-reliance.

An important piece of advice from Fiona Adler, entrepreneur and the third Australian woman to reach the summit of Everest, was to avoid unhelpful labels. She recalls:

> *People should avoid boxing themselves in too much. It's good to know yourself and know where your tendencies lie. You can put a positive spin on [your tendencies] whichever way you look at it. People might think that you're a dreamer, but really you're a big thinker. One of my old teachers from high school said, 'You're always stubborn.' I thought, well... actually, I'm persistent. You can look at any trait in either a negative or a positive way.*

Fiona, having started multiple new start-ups and having climbed Everest, is a master of managing her thinking and beliefs. This ability to notice and actively work with your thoughts and inner voices gives you the freedom to choose and amplify the thoughts that help you to move forward.

Negotiate with your inner voices

How often do you hold back, not because of what others say, but what you say to yourself? Have you ever had critical voices telling you that you should or shouldn't be doing something? Have your voices told you off for making a mistake or not being perfect? If you've ever been affected by the impostor syndrome or perfectionism, you know that your inner critic is rather harsh. This inner critic says that you don't know enough, you don't deserve to be where you are and that you'll be 'found out'.

If you actively listen to some of your inner voices – the helpful and not so helpful ones – you'll start to identify the ones that affect you more than others. If you have positive inner voices that support you to grow and challenge yourself, fantastic! Keep those with you as you'll need them when you face obstacles or when things don't go to plan.

Then there are the unhelpful, negative and critical voices. Have you ever tried to ignore and eliminate them or talk over them with positive thinking? Sometimes this works but the effects don't last because they find a way to rear their heads again. It's like playing those Whac-A-Mole games. We need to create a different relationship with these negative inner voices.

A strategy that's worked for me and for people I've coached involves a method adapted from process-oriented psychology, which is a field of psychology that facilitates personal development and evolution. Essentially, the trick is to consciously interact with the voice until it has less power over you.

First, identify a few negative inner voices that hold you back. They tend to be ones that start with:

- I'll never…
- I always…
- I'm too…
- I should…
- I shouldn't…
- I can't…

They could be based on conditioning and internalised marginalisation, as described in Chapter 7. They may be voices based on beliefs such as:

- Quiet people are never considered for leadership positions.
- Self-promotion is for braggers and attention seekers… 'I'm Asian, you know, we're brought up to be humble.'
- Women have less confidence than men, and that's why they don't put their hands up for promotions.

- You'll be seen as incompetent unless you have fully formed, well-considered ideas before speaking up.

These beliefs can end up as negative and unhelpful inner voices. When repeated enough, they become a reality in your mind, and you act as if they were true. These voices will play in your mind like a broken record:

- 'I'm too quiet to be a leader, I won't bother trying.'
- 'I can't do self-promotion, it makes me uncomfortable and I'm not very good at it.'
- 'I'm not confident in putting myself forward for promotions.'
- 'I can't speak up; I don't have anything to add because I haven't thought it through yet.'

Choose one of these negatives to work on first, you may wish to pick the most persistent one.

The second step involves distancing yourself from the voice so that it's not a part of you. Imagine someone else is saying these things to you. Visualise the inner critic who is telling you these things and how.

The third step is to interact with the voice. You could get curious and ask questions, push back on their criticisms, tell them that the current approach is not working and eventually negotiate a different way of relating.

The easiest way to do this exercise, especially when starting up, is with a friend or colleague who can act out the interaction with the voice with you. Someone who is a good negotiator or mediator would be of great help. Your job is to become the unhelpful, negative and critical voice: the same voice that plays in your head. If it's a nagging voice, talk with a nagging voice. If it's an authoritative, punitive voice, use that. Your friend's job is to interact with this voice and negotiate to find a better approach.

My own experience

One of the voices that used to play repeatedly in my mind was, 'Don't do anything that makes you stand out. You'll be persecuted!'

This voice stemmed from a range of experiences of being picked on as a child because I was a bit different. I stood out in Australia because I was one of very few Asian kids in an Australian public school. I stood out in Japan because I was one of very few children who had lived overseas. Some of the teachers and children were welcoming of my differences, but others were very unkind, like the ones I shared in the introduction. There were plenty of other instances, like when a younger school child threw rocks at me and said, 'Go back to where you came from' at a school in Adelaide, or when a Japanese girl at school deliberately gave me the wrong information so I would miss the English speaking club classes in grade 7. Combined with this was the conditioning from growing up in a collectivist Japanese culture in my teenage years when I just wanted desperately to fit in.

So, when I started Quietly Powerful in 2016, I was petrified to share, even though it was something I believed would help people. It was something that no one in Australia was doing, which would mean standing out and being the centre of attention. And you know how much I don't like being the centre of attention!

I remember when I told a few colleagues that I was thinking of running public breakfasts to share the ideas. I felt shy, my face went red and I giggled nervously as if I was about to go on my first date. The 'don't stand out' voice was telling me that I should be careful and that I should worry about the reactions I might get from people.

In this situation, what I did with my inner voice was to first distance myself from it. This particular voice, I discovered, was a protective voice: 'Don't do that, you're going to get criticised and judged. You're going to stand out and people aren't going to like it. They'll pull you down! You know what that's like, you've been there before.'

Step two was to call on the negotiator. The negotiator voice said, 'What makes you think that people will pull her down? I know that happened when Megumi was in school, but that was 30 years ago, she's grown up now.' My protector voice might reply, 'You know what people are like when they see someone doing something different. It's no different to school days. It's dangerous. I don't want her to get hurt again.' The negotiator responded with, 'I get that you're trying to protect Megumi, but you're holding her back. Can we work out another way you can help?'

After a few iterations you'll find the negative inner voice will start to lose power. You might find that there's a particular phrase that diminishes its power. It won't go away completely, but it won't drive you as much as it did.

The best thing that worked for me was to reassure the protective voice by telling it something like, 'I'll be okay, it won't be the end of the world,' and, 'If I don't do it, I'll regret it so I have to have a go.' Even now, whenever the protective voice pops up to warn me, I use these phrases to counter it and stop it from taking over my thinking.

If you can catch these thoughts and beliefs, you can consciously develop a different relationship with them. Longstanding beliefs may take some time and effort to overcome, but the more you use the phrases to diminish their power, the stronger the neural pathways become. You *can* reduce the impact of these voices.

The process of understanding yourself is never-ending, but the more you try, the more your self-acceptance grows and allows you to be comfortable in your own skin.

3. Leverage your uniqueness strategically

When you have a range of qualities that are both strengths and weaknesses, you can start to strategically use them in ways that are useful. The qualities that you once thought were weaknesses can become your greatest asset. If they're qualities that aren't often seen in your team or organisation, they'll be your greatest differentiator and competitive advantage.

Many of the Quietly Powerful leaders I spoke with have shared how they have leveraged their unique qualities and shared invaluable tips and advice.

Helen Macfarlane, Partner at Addisons, spoke about how her quiet nature became an advantage. She recalls:

...sometimes [what] people might do with quiet achievers is underestimate their ambition. It may not be so overt. Just because somebody is quiet, [it] doesn't mean they're not confident. I think quieter people might not talk as frequently, but often, when they do speak, [their comments and observations] can be absolute gems because they have the time to actually think.

Being underestimated has some benefits in the right context. When people aren't expecting you to say a lot, the novelty and surprise of you speaking can cause people to listen more and this can help your insights have a bigger impact.

Dr Jason Fox learned how to not only use his distinct qualities but amplify them, which makes him memorable as a speaker. He said:

I do feel as though when you're speaking on stage it's a performance role. There's theatre to it. You are stepping into a role that 'requires a sense of amplified authenticity' (to quote Matt Church of Thought Leaders Business School). I try not to get too self-attached, but there are certain things that serve well. For me, the introversion becomes amplified, my academic nature turns into something wizardly. It's an amplified persona – nothing is faked: I'm just bringing more of a particular aspect of my 'self'.

In the world of professional speaking, where there are countless captivating speakers with stories of tragedy, adversity and triumph, Jason has been able to stand out with his unique perspectives and style.

Susan Middleditch, who has been in multiple senior roles in government and corporates, uses her strengths in one-on-one relationships to influence people around critical decisions before group meetings. She said:

> *I think another approach that works is that I'm better off one-on-one than I am in a really big group setting. That allows me to understand where they're coming from and what their concerns [might] be, as well as being able to provide my view before I walk into the room and try and get a collective view before arguing it all out [with everyone] across the table.*

Many people believe that you need to be a persuasive speaker to have influence. Susan's approach demonstrates how the opposite approach can bring people along more than people potentially feeling coerced through persuasion. While it may require some investment upfront, it's a more informed and collaborative approach to making decisions and gains more support in the long run.

Anne Flanagan, former CFO at RACV, shared that she preferred English to maths and sciences at school but ended up in finance because her parents wanted her to be financially independent. She now appreciates how she can use her natural interest and affinity with storytelling to convert finance into plain-English. She has found that this combined skill has been an advantage for her career progression. She said:

> *I often think that one of the reasons I've managed to be successful is that I've chosen a field where communication skills are not necessarily commonplace and so if you've got that ability to tell a story and convert finance into English, people listen and it gives you a chance to succeed... finance isn't about the list of numbers, it's about doing the analysis and telling the story... creating a story about the organisation.*

When Michelle Grocock isn't playing the executive general manager role, she trains as an Ironman. She said that there are many introverts in endurance sports, and she believes it is because of their quiet determination. She said:

> ... *if I think of the characteristics of endurance sports, yes, fitness is part of it, but so much of it is mental. It's determination, never giving up, no excuses. In an Ironman Triathlon, where you're out on the bike for six hours and running for four or five hours, you've got to get used to your own company. It's that quiet, relentless determination that I think powers people.*

You can see from these examples that when you're comfortable with your own nature, you can use it to your advantage as well as to benefit the people you work with. You become the instrument for the work you do, and the best music is created from playing the instrument as it was supposed to be played.

Chapter 17

Adapt purposefully

Adapting purposefully, the second part to developing as a Quietly Powerful leader, is ensuring that you have something meaningful that pulls you towards growing and adapting. This meaning gives you the energy and courage to break out of your comfort zone to do something you've never done before.

The strategy of adapting purposefully draws on the psychological Free Trait theory. If you like, your actions and behaviours are driven by love rather than fear such that you *have* do it, even if it's uncomfortable.

This chapter covers the steps and lessons from the Quietly Powerful leader interviewees as well as additional resources you could access to adapt purposefully. I hope it helps you to get started on the process.

Adapting purposefully involves three major steps:

1. Committing to a worthwhile mission.
2. Adjusting yourself and your surroundings.
3. Cultivating your Quietly Powerful presence.

Three steps to adapting purposefully

	LIMITING	THRIVING
Understand + Reframe + Leverage (Appreciate fully)	SHRINKING	FAKING

Adapt purposefully

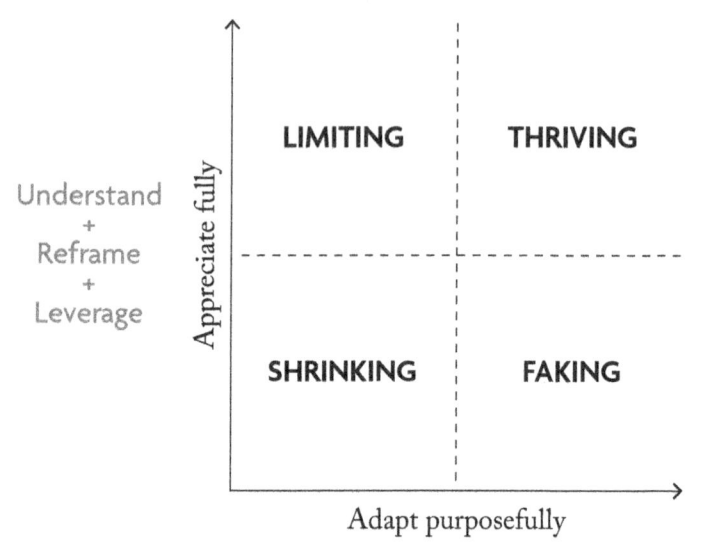

MISSION + PRESENCE + ADJUSTMENTS

1. Commit to a worthwhile mission

Most people who are naturally quiet don't like being the centre of attention. Actions, which draw attention to themselves, such as speaking up in a group, public speaking, putting their hand up for senior leadership positions and promoting themselves feel awkward or even frightening. The following Quietly Powerful leaders show how they were able to stretch themselves to do things they felt uncomfortable with, because they felt compelled by a powerful purpose and mission.

Susan Middleditch, Deputy Secretary of Victoria Police, and Michelle Grocock, Executive General Manager, Internal Audit at National Australia Bank said similar things about speaking up in meetings.

Susan said she used to sit back and listen, such that her ideas were never shared, or they were shared too late. She eventually had to convince herself that there was a good reason why she was hired and was invited to the meeting in the first place. She had a more people-oriented perspective to contribute to meetings where it was not the usual consideration. With her passion for people and culture, she overcame her anxiety about speaking up. Over time, she became more comfortable with speaking up about what she cared about.

Similarly, Michelle Grocock is known for speaking up a lot in meetings when she is passionate about the topic. She said:

I do tend to have strong views, but it's because the topics I'm involved in I'm incredibly passionate about. And therefore, any reluctance to speak up is overcome by a determination to make a difference. I'm at the point now where if I don't speak up about something I see or something I believe in, I feel like I've let myself down and not done my job... I often get told that I'm the person in any meeting who will speak up about things that everybody else is thinking but isn't asking.

For both Susan and Michelle, aligning themselves and their work to their values and passions, and committing to making a difference in these areas, has allowed them to express their views when needed.

Ruth Picker, mentioned in Chapter 13, found the courage to do something she had never done before, even when she didn't know how to start. It was in 2013 that she decided to reconnect with her passion and become a songwriter. She had learned music and composition as a young person in South Africa but had not written music for 33 years.

What prompted her to reconnect with and share her musical passion was a personal reason. She said:

...the real impetus [was when] my cousin's wife, Merle, passed away. She was diagnosed with breast cancer on the same day as me. She was operated on the same day as me and she died three months later. And on the day that she died, I couldn't sleep...

> *My whole family were just in such shock. I couldn't sleep, I got up, I went to the keyboard and I wrote the song for Merle. I sent the words to Michael, [my cousin], that night and he read it as the eulogy at her funeral. When he came to Melbourne later that year, I played him the melody on the piano and he said, 'Please will you record this song for me?' I thought, I can't give this man his wife back, but I can give him this song, and it can be on the record.*

Ruth didn't know how she would record the song, but she told her cousin that she would. She eventually figured out how to record the music, and then she started writing and recording other songs after that. She then founded The Song Tailors with the intention of providing an ongoing platform for emerging and established artists to prosper in the creative industry. She never thought it was something that could be combined with her professional side and she was pleasantly surprised when her managers at Ernst & Young were happy to support her being a songwriter while also working as a Partner at the firm. She said:

> *I was actually afraid to [ask] because I thought they'd say no. But their response was the opposite, their response was, 'Wow, that's amazing.' They loved what I was doing, and they loved that it was supporting the creative industry, both emerging and established. Then they said, 'You're actually setting an example about being authentic and bringing your whole self to work.'*

Her passion for music and purpose of supporting emerging artists enabled her to step outside of her comfort zone. She's now comfortable with her dual identity of Partner at Ernst & Young and songwriter, and is an inspiration for many people.

What kind of purpose, mission or passion pulls you? How do you find one?

Of course, it would be powerful to have a big, life-size mission or purpose that you are so committed to that you stretch yourself beyond what you thought you were capable of. Greta Thunberg and Rosa Parks, as mentioned in Chapter 1, are perfect examples of quiet people taking on a big mission to change the world in their own way.

For many of us, at a practical level, this mission or purpose doesn't necessarily have to be life-size or global. It can be smaller things that are causing us problems or frustrations, such as stakeholders on a project who are holding us up by not talking with each other to resolve their differences. It can be a passion to help others, such as empowering more women to be financially fit, or it can be a commitment to helping organisations, like advocating ethical decision-making.

When you care enough about these problems or passions and you commit to doing something, you can step up and take the lead.

The following questions could help you to start identifying some meaningful missions:

- **Strengths:** What are your natural strengths? What comes easily to you that others find difficult? What expertise do you have that others don't?

- **Passions:** What are you passionate about? What makes your heart sing? What makes your blood boil (makes you angry, frustrated, annoyed)? What's something you wished was different at work, at home or in the world?

- **Adding value:** Where do you think you can add value to areas like the workplace, family, community or the world? Of the various things you do, what is valued by others? What value do you bring that others commented on?

If you look back at the stories shared about Susan Middleditch, Michelle Grocock and Ruth Picker, you will find that they tapped into a strength and expertise they had – something they were passionate about – which added value to others.

When you start answering these questions you will find that your focus shifts from your own concerns to bigger concerns beyond yourself. That's what pulls you to do what you've never done before and keeps you going. That's why Quietly Powerful leaders are purposeful. They lead because they can see how by stepping into leadership they can make a difference.

2. Adjust yourself and your surroundings

Stacey Barr, mentioned in Chapter 13, shared that she was an incredibly shy person and found it difficult to get her messages across to people. It was when she realised that she had a message worth sharing that she decided to adapt herself to speak up. Her tips are relevant whether you are doing a presentation, going into a meeting, influencing people on a project or helping people to understand what you know and do well. She said:

> *I think of three things. One is [to] go and watch some of those TED talks or read some of those books and realise that it's not a valid belief that just because you're quiet, you can't be successful. The second thing would be [to] get really clear about what message you do want to get out there and practise it a little bit and prepare yourself. The third is to overcome the fear of actually having a go, treat it like an experiment. Each time you're going to a meeting, or go to a presentation, or turn up in a group, think about the message that you want to get across; how you want to do it. Frame it as an experiment and do it. And then decide: did it work? Didn't it work? What have I learned? What would I do differently next time? Don't die in a ditch over every single interaction being perfectly successful.*

Just like Stacey, the other Quietly Powerful leaders shared what they found challenging and how they had to adjust their behaviours to serve the role they were taking up. Their stories are around some of the most common challenges for quiet professionals: managing perceptions, speaking up, increasing visibility and networking. I also explore how you can adjust to your surroundings and find ways to encourage others to adjust.

Managing perceptions

Being misunderstood is a common challenge for quiet professionals. Because of your quiet approach, you may be seen as disengaged, uncommitted, at times incompetent or that you have nothing to add. Quietly Powerful leaders described ways in which they had to address these perceptions by adjusting their approach.

Dianne Jacobs described the challenges for quiet professionals as a perception gap, particularly when they're with people who don't know them well. Others can misinterpret your quieter approach as a lack of energy and commitment, or they might misunderstand how you've come to a particular point of view.

Susan Allen had to watch out for her tendency to walk straight past people when she was deep in thought, especially as she became more senior in organisations. She found that unless she looked up and smiled at people in the corridor, people misunderstood and thought that she was unhappy with them.

Susan Middleditch realised that she had to share more of herself as she took on senior roles where larger teams reported to her. She found it difficult, as it felt like she was exposing herself. However, she worked at it as she knew it was important for her to be approachable and connect with people without necessarily having one-on-one relationships. She learned to be a more human leader by sharing her imperfections and things that were going on outside of work as well. She said:

> *It was when I moved to an agency where I did have a really large team. I couldn't have the one-on-one relationships with my team members, which is what I was used to. I found out that my team members didn't know who I was and so [they] couldn't connect with me. I had to find different ways to be able to show them that I was approachable. I really felt like I was exposing myself and it took a lot of effort for me to do that. [I used] reminders to make sure that I took the time to say hello. When I do [group] forums I try and put little stories in about whatever's going on in my*

life or with my kids. Very early on, that was very difficult because that's not something that I thought a leader had to do.

Ruth Picker talked about how being a petite woman made it difficult for to be seen and heard earlier in her career:

Because I was quiet and because I was small, I had the double combination of being below eyeline. People wouldn't even see me, never mind hear me. So, my challenge was being small, being quietly spoken and being overlooked – and often.

She shared a strategy to overcome her disadvantage – to make a good second impression. She worked on making sure that the first thing she said in any meeting was powerful and impactful. She would listen carefully and think about what would add value to the conversation. When it worked, it was as if people saw her for the first time, thinking, *Who is that person I hadn't seen over there…?*

It takes courage and effort to make sure you're seen and heard when you start from behind – whether it's because you're small, a woman, quiet, culturally different from the group or feel like an outsider.

Becoming more aware of others' perceptions of you and the impact of these perceptions is key to starting the process of addressing those that hold you back. Therefore, asking for feedback from people you know well and people who are new to you are both useful.

While it's easy to blame others for misunderstanding you, it would be much more effective to identify what's creating the misunderstandings and work on small steps to address the misperceptions. Finding your own way to speak up and be heard is an important adjustment to make.

Speaking up

Simon Harrington, first mentioned in Chapter 2, talked about his dislike of big forums when there was a debate, especially if he was one of the more junior members. He experienced occasions where he saw others being ignored or shut down by those who were more senior or had strong opinions.

Since retiring from the Navy, Simon has been doing a lot of coaching and mentoring. He's now learned some techniques which he thinks would have helped him to speak up and be heard. He said:

> *I would advise someone to introduce [their opinion] by saying, 'Look I don't think a lot of people are going to agree with me here, but I think this is something that does need to be considered,' and [finishing with] 'what am I missing?' [You need to] break the people in, rather than just throwing the dead cat on the table. [You need to] say, 'I'm going to throw a dead cat on the table somehow. Here's the dead cat. Why is it dead?' I think that will help people come back and listen to you a bit better than they might otherwise.*

Oscar Trimboli used to hold back from sharing his thinking until it was fully formed. He used to speak up at the last few minutes of a meeting after having heard and considered multiple internal and external variables across time and context. He was then considered a 'terrorist' because it was like he was throwing hand grenades at the end of the dialogue, blowing up everyone's thinking that had been shared to that point.

His manager encouraged him to speak up earlier and told him that the others were missing out when he didn't share his insights early enough in conversations. He said:

> *That fantastic manager, took me aside and said, 'If you haven't spoken in the first 15 minutes of the one-hour meeting or the first ten minutes of the 30-minute meeting, just use this phrase: "My idea isn't fully formed. Is it okay if I share it with the group?"'*

When he started to share his thoughts earlier in this way, he realised that not only did people welcome his perspectives, nine times out of ten his ideas were more formed than what the group had been discussing.

Michelle Grocock shared her strategy of preparing herself and keeping herself actively engaged in conversations by pretending that someone could ask her a question at any moment in time. She said:

> *I would always be sitting in those meetings thinking, 'What is the question I want to ask? What is my view on something?' It actually became quite a good habit to get myself into, because then in your own brain you can be thinking about, 'What is the question I would have asked?' And then start to practise actually asking it.*

In my Quietly Powerful coaching groups, many of the participants find speaking up challenging. What I've been encouraging them to experiment with is speaking even when they don't feel they have comment to add. For example, you can contribute by asking a question that no one has asked. This adds value and can sometimes be the turning point in conversations. Another example would be to use your strength in listening and observation to share a summary of what you've heard so far, just as Michelle Grocock does. She told me:

> *I seemed to have fallen into quite a natural role of letting the extroverts talk, but to be the person who brings it all together. They might talk a lot, but they're heading in different directions and they don't actually do anything as a result of the talking. I'm the one who then steps in and says, 'Okay, so based on what I've heard, I think I've heard this, this and this, and I think we should do that, that, and that.'*

Liz Compton also uses the summarising technique a lot. She finds that it adds great value to conversation by pausing and summarising for the group, so they can be clearer about their next steps. She also added:

> *Don't be afraid of pausing the conversation. Even if the conversation has moved on, pause and say 'I've got something else to raise here… it's not quite thought through yet, but I can share now, or I can come back to it in a few minutes.'*

This summarising strategy is helpful for many quiet professionals who find that the conversation moves on before they can add their point.

Increasing visibility

Many quiet professionals are told to be 'more visible' to progress in their careers. Self-promotion is difficult and awkward for most people, but is particularly tough for quiet professionals.

Caroline Stainkamph used to wonder why no one was noticing her achievements when she was doing good work. She realised that people simply didn't notice because they were busy. She recalled:

> *The fact is that everyone's busy, and you need to promote yourself. It doesn't have to be in a loud, vivacious 'Look at me, here I am!' way. You can promote yourself in quiet ways. It's making sure that you're telling people what you're doing. You also need to tell your boss about the good work that you're doing, because they're busy too. Make sure you build a network of people – of supporters – and make sure they know what you're doing.*

Dianne Jacobs, who coaches senior leaders to be ready to sit on boards, also encourages people to let others know what they are working on, even during informal conversations. She said:

> *The visibility part comes about by making sure that people know what you're working on. Even common questions like, 'How are you?' doesn't have to [be met] with 'I'm fine'. Instead, it can be a response of, 'I'm doing some interesting work at the moment,' and you [can] tell them about a project or a certain aspect of your*

work that might be important. Make the effort to actually 'tell and share' relevant activities.

She also shared that visibility and self-promotion can be reframed so that it's a two-way exchange of ideas. She said:

Tell people what you're doing, and it has lovely benefits… it's a way of forming a connection based on ideas because what you can then say is, 'What are your experiences with this? Have you ever come across it? Have you thought about it before?' So it becomes an exchange of ideas and information. Self-promotion really is about the tell rather than the sell, and a way of engaging other people around mutual interests and benefits.

Clive Peter provided some advice on how you might inform others of what you're doing and achieving by linking it to your accountabilities. He suggested that by sharing what you are accountable for, and asking others to reinforce what is important, you can clarify that you own the work. You can also be bold and courageous upfront by putting your hand up to own a project or outcome so that it's clear that you took ownership and delivered. In addition, by partnering with the right people to deliver results, you can be recognised by those partners and through acknowledging each other's contributions.

Clive also cautioned against using your quietness or your introversion as an excuse:

Just because you're introverted or quiet doesn't mean you shouldn't work on being able to speak publicly. It shouldn't mean you don't work hard on engaging a group. You do need to be prepared to be courageous.

Elizabeth Proust also explained that working hard and expecting people to notice doesn't work. Her suggestion is to put your hand up to contribute your skills and experiences so that more people can see first-hand what you can bring. She said:

> *I think that the natural style for quieter people is to think, well, if I just put my head down and keep working hard that will be noticed. Unfortunately, that's not usually the case. So, networking is important, and I don't mean necessarily drinks after work on a Friday night, I'm thinking more networking with professional people, being on a panel at a conference, putting yourself out there to do something, putting your hand up at work to lead a project. I think all of those things, when the opportunity arises, think about what skills and experiences you can bring and then put yourself forward.*

One of the tips I give people who struggle with self-promotion is to reframe it to being about sharing something important beyond themselves. When I feel hesitant about promoting my work on Quietly Powerful, I remind myself that it's not about me, it's about the people I help with my messages.

Both Fiona Adler and Dr Jenny Brockis shared the same tip. Fiona had to promote herself in growing her start-up businesses and found a way to reframe self-promotion as something beyond herself. She said that what worked for her was to show enthusiasm by thinking of herself as an advocate for her team and her customers. Similarly, Dr Jenny Brockis got advice from a mentor to remind herself to promote the value she provides, the messages she shares and their benefits. She could then tap into her passion for helping people to improve their brain health and enjoy smarter thinking.

Quietly Powerful leaders have worked out that you can increase your visibility by sharing what you're working on and what you're achieving – whether through a conversation that's helpful to others, or by asking for advice or through a visual tool. It's also helpful to reframe the purpose of self-promotion and increasing your visibility. It's a way to connect with people, exchange ideas, share information that's useful to others or to promote your team, your customers and your organisation.

Something that's worked for me when I've found myself shrinking in a cloud of 'I don't want to put myself out there', has been to tell myself that I had to share something, because it could be useful to others. Like Dianne, Fiona and Jenny's advice to reframe, I regularly work on reframing visibility as part of serving a bigger mission.

Networking

When I ask whether people find networking difficult or exhausting at my Quietly Powerful events, about 90 per cent of the hands go up.

Quietly Powerful leaders are no different. Some still find it exhausting, but they've found ways to make it easier while also expanding their thinking surrounding networking.

Clive Peter still finds it difficult and feels shy going into new settings where he doesn't know anybody. Some of the ways he makes it easier for himself are:

> *Thinking it through, doing homework and knowing who's going to be there. If I know who's at the meeting I've looked them up on LinkedIn, or to see if I know anybody else just to have that common ground or to bring a great wing person with me.*

'Taking a friend' is a strategy that Helen Macfarlane encourages as well, now that she's become more comfortable with attending functions. She said:

> *I encourage members of the team to network or attend functions and make sure they have a wingman to help them break the ice, especially when they're not comfortable going to a function where they don't know anyone. I encourage them to attend with me because it's something that they'll become much more confident in doing, particularly if they're going to an event where they don't know anyone.*

Helen has become more comfortable with networking by using an approach that works for her. She uses her strength in building one-on-one relationships by approaching and being friendly to people who are standing by themselves.

Aneetha de Silva isn't shy about engaging with people, she'll happily initiate a conversation. She does, however, prefer, and actively looks for, smaller groups. She said:

In a more formal meeting setting, in a large industry event, I'll tend to look for the smaller groups to have my conversations with. I definitely enjoy and find it more meaningful to talk in a smaller group than in larger groups where you run into a small talk really quickly... Because I like connecting with people, I find it much easier to have a genuine conversation in a smaller group.

I still find networking functions exhausting, especially when they are missing a purpose or topic that brings people together. So, I only tend to go to functions where there's a speaker or topic that I find interesting.

In addition, I also remind my coaching clients that networking is not just about going to functions. The purpose of networking is to build a network of people who you could support or could support you. I encourage my clients to find ways to be introduced to people by people they already know. It may seem like a slow process, but it's actually more meaningful and the introductions make it ten times easier to have conversations.

You can see that there are many ways to adjust your approach or reframe your thinking so that you can be seen, heard and recognised. Making these adjustments doesn't change who you are, it just adds to your repertoire of skills and behaviours. When you make these adjustments to fulfil a purpose, you are truly stepping into leadership in your own authentic way.

To make adjustments and build skills, practice is key. If you start small and build on it, your comfort zone will expand. You don't need to be comfortable when you start, and indeed, you may never be fully comfortable. You just need courage to start and keep at it.

Adjusting your surroundings

A young woman told me about a time when she applied for a job when she was just starting her professional career. She told the interview panel that she was an introvert and that she needed time and space to think. Sadly, she didn't get the job. While she is not entirely sure that telling them about her introversion contributed to her not getting the job, she had a feeling that it did.

One of the realisations I've had over the past few years is that it's not worth trying too hard to please people, teams and organisations if they're not even going to give you a chance. There will be others who do, and it's worth the effort when they can see the value you could bring through your natural qualities.

I've been fortunate enough to have clients who valued my quieter approach to consulting and facilitation, particularly once they experienced the benefits. I've then been able to request taking approaches that work for me. For example, I've asked a client to give me some time to think about a problem or a question rather than giving them my immediate thoughts. I've also requested workshops be designed in ways so that I have sufficient recovery time. Most of the time, clients have no problem with accommodating my requests, as they're aware that it's the best way to get value from me. Some of my clients know me so well now that they'll ask me, 'Would you like to think about that for a few days?'

If you're aware of what affects your performance, you can take responsibility to ensure that everything is set up in ways that work for you.

Fiona Adler found that in starting up her business, Word of Mouth, she built up a sales and customer service team to the extent that it turned into a small call centre. She found it exhausting managing such a team and she had to find ways to fit in recovery time. She said:

> *Basically, what started as an idea for a great website that everyone can use, turned into running a small call centre. I felt that quite challenging because, in a way, you're just running this very noisy [workplace]. After doing that all day and then also coming home to noisy kids who haven't seen me, [I was exhausted]. I was trying to find little pockets of quiet time, like going for a walk at lunchtime and cherishing the evening times a little bit where I tried to do more of my thinking work.*

Many quiet professionals need that quiet recovery time and, as Fiona said, you will need to create the recovering time deliberately.

Katrina Webb, mentioned in Chapter 6, describes self-care as part of her work. She prioritises her time to ensure that she has downtime and time for herself so she can be her best self. She said:

> *What is a non-negotiable for me is my self-care and the way I manage my energy. That not only includes what I fuel my body with, it includes the amount of sleep I get and rest I get during the day. It's about looking at what activities actually re-energise me physically and mentally. Is that with people or not with people? Does that mean I need to exercise or not? It's different for everyone. [Self-care] is a part of my working week, that I invest in my energy management, and it becomes a meeting in my diary with myself.*

Seeing recovery time as part of your work is a reframe that allows you to treat it as essential. You can schedule time for this so that it doesn't become a low priority.

Aneetha de Silva also supported the view that choosing the right environment and people to work with was important. She said:

> *It's really important to keep doing things that make you confident. Find people who you know will support you, both directly and indirectly. Don't take jobs where you know you're not going to be*

set up for success because it's terribly difficult to recover from them. One of my learnings is that it's not always the job that matters but the people around you because they make you succeed.

Adjust yourself and your surroundings so that the best of you can shine and people get your best contribution. It will take effort to adjust yourself but remember that it's in service of your mission and purpose, whatever you choose that to be.

3. Cultivate your Quietly Powerful presence

People can feel your presence long before you speak.

You may have experienced someone walking into a room where you felt the energy drop. Or someone else arriving and you felt the energy lift. What kind of presence do people feel when you walk into a room? Do people feel at ease with you or do they sense anxiety?

The HeartMath Institute has been studying heart neurons and their electromagnetic field. The heart's electromagnetic field can be measured anywhere on the surface of the body and also several feet away from the body. So, it's true that your presence can be felt. If you've ever been in the presence of a spiritual leader with a powerful presence, you know what a quietly powerful presence *could* be like.

The final piece of the puzzle for becoming Quietly Powerful is to develop your quietly powerful presence. A lot of what has been covered so far will help you to grow into such a presence. Appreciating yourself fully is essential to becoming comfortable in your own skin, which people can sense when they meet you. When you're comfortable, you're able to be more present in the moment without being distracted by your inner voices. When you gain new skills and behaviours and become comfortable with them over time, you also build a quietly confident presence.

What can fast-track this development, however, is to work on your presence from the inside out and outside in.

Work from the inside out

Your presence is affected by what you pay attention to. If you're stewing over the past, like something you said that you wished you hadn't, you aren't present. If you're worrying about the future, like a difficult meeting coming up, you aren't present. When you're speaking with someone, your mind may already be formulating your response. In that moment, you weren't present and you missed what they said. Often your mind wanders uncontrollably. Some of you may think that it cannot be controlled because it just happens.

Practising mindfulness and meditation trains your mind to be in control of what you give your attention to. Regular practice enables you to catch yourself when your mind wanders and you can bring your attention back to where you want it to be.

The most incredible gift you can give someone is your presence. That's incredibly hard to do if you don't learn how to calm your nervous system down.
—Dr Mark Hyman, MD

You can work on growing your quietly powerful presence from the inside out by doing simple breathing techniques to practising meditation every day. There are many meditation teachers, courses and apps these days, some of which are supported by scientific research, others based on ancient traditions. If you've never done it before, you can start small and try a five-minute meditation using a meditation app. As you get used to it, you can increase the time and do it more frequently.

Personally, I know that meditating every day for the last 18 years has had an enormous impact on my ability to manage my thoughts. Regular meditation has also built up a memory of the calming effect of breathing, so I have become more effective at accessing my calm state by focusing on my breath.

Katrina Webb has worked closely with psychologists over the years and is a yoga practitioner. She also talked about breath as an important tool for maintaining her calm and choosing her responses consciously:

> *We were born with the mechanics of knowing how to breathe properly, yet stress in life has changed our mechanics of breathing. We've actually forgotten how to breathe properly. The longer we can inhale and exhale, the longer we live. Breath is a free tool, yet most of us don't tap into the power of the breath. If you're about to be triggered emotionally, and then go into physical reaction, there's that space [to use considered breathing]. Psychologists told me, in the research I've done, that breath is the only known tool that lowers our cortisol, which is our stress hormone.*

I also encourage people to 'have a smile on the inside'; it brings up feelings of contentment and peace. Taoist Master, Mantak Chia, has taught the practice of 'inner smile' for over four decades. He says that in ancient China, the Taoists believed that a constant inner smile ensured health, happiness and longevity. Some Buddhists teach the inner smile as well. Have a go, you'll feel the effects almost straight away by simply imagining a smile on the inside. You might find that your face softens and smiles gently as well.

When you feel quietly powerful on the inside, you can just be, you don't need anything from anyone, and you don't need to show or prove how powerful you are on the outside.

Work from the outside in

In March 2017, I was invited to speak about Quietly Powerful at an Importance of Women breakfast hosted by Vic ICT for Women, a not-for-profit organisation that champions women in STEM. Caroline Stainkamph, mentioned in Chapters 12 and 13, managed these breakfasts and invited me to speak at one of them. She had spoken about her leadership journey, including a story about when she discovered she was an introvert, so I was excited to follow her lead and share my story.

A few days before the breakfast, I received an email from the organisers: 'We have a new record for IOW [Importance of Women breakfast] registrations with 120 online bookings. Registrations closed at around 12:23pm today.' My heart jumped, partly due to excitement and partly due to anxiety due to high expectations.

I thought I was pretty good at managing my nerves before presentations. I've been meditating for 18 years, right? And I've been facilitating workshops and presenting to groups for about the same amount of time. I should be used to it. That morning, however, I was nervous. It was the first time I spoke to such a large audience about Quietly Powerful and I felt a sense of obligation to so many people who registered.

I got up early to meditate in the morning and I did my usual deep breathing when I arrived in the room. I still felt a knot in my stomach. Some of the old inner voices started creeping up, 'What are you doing speaking to over 100 people? What if they don't like what you say? What if you forget what to say?'

These are the moments when you need several tricks up your sleeve. My inside-out strategies were not quite enough. I went to the bathroom and had a moment to chat to my inner voices. 'It's not the end of the world, even if I stuff up. It will be okay.' I then stood tall with my chest lifted in a classical ballet pose with a gentle smile. I breathed deeply a few more times in this pose. I was ready.

The outside-in approach is to use your physiology and movement to influence your psychology.

Amy Cuddy, author of *Presence* and a social psychologist from the Harvard Business School, found through her own research and 55 other studies, that adopting an expansive posture makes people feel more powerful. Cuddy popularised 'power posing' in her TED talk in 2012, which she now calls *postural feedback*.

Cuddy demonstrates her power pose like Wonder Woman with her fists on her hips. The Wonder Woman pose didn't work for me so I found my own pose, which was the classical ballet pose. I felt more of a connection to this pose as I've been enjoying adult ballet classes since 2016. I suggest to people that they find their own poses that work for them. Some people do other forms of dance or sports and will intuitively know a pose that gives them a feeling of strength and calm.

In fact, Cuddy says, 'Expanding your body language – through posture, movement, and speech – makes you feel more confident and powerful, less anxious and self-absorbed, and generally more positive.' So, you can use movement and speech just as much as posture. This explained why I felt so much more positive and uplifted after adult ballet classes. The physical posture and movement altered my hormonal balance and psychology.

Susan Allen found public speaking daunting and had to find ways to become more present on stage. She found herself feeling self-conscious, which took her away from being present with the audience. She said that one of the things that worked for her was to work on her physical posture:

> *I actually did a course at NIDA [National Institute of Dramatic Art] a while ago. They use the techniques of acting to teach you how to project your voice. One of my favourites is 'the cape, crown and headlight exercise'. Apparently, Cate Blanchett uses it before she walks on stage. You have to imagine you have a cape around your shoulders, which pulls your shoulders back, and you have to imagine you've got a crown on your head. So, that brings your chin in and lengthens your spine. And then you've got a headlight in the middle of your chest, and then you walk into the room. It makes a huge difference.*

You can also try smiling by thinking of a place, something or someone you love, which is an outside-in and inside-out approach. Research shows that smiling has physiological and psychological effects. It has positive health effects, such as lowering heart rate and blood pressure, too.

By working from the inside out and outside in, we can develop a quietly powerful presence. This presence is far more powerful than the dominant, powering over presence, as it allows others to connect and be with you, rather than feeling afraid or disconnected from you. Amy Cuddy said, 'when you become present, you allow others to be present. Presence doesn't make you dominant in an alpha sense; it actually allows you to hear other people. And for them to feel heard.' This is the kind of leadership presence we want and need more of.

~

Quietly Powerful leadership is powerful in ways that other styles are not. As a quiet professional, there are many ways in which you can use your quiet nature to your leadership advantage. You can fully utilise these advantages by moving yourself from feeling quietly disempowered to Quietly Powerful. It takes personal development from the inside out, not just quick fixes with tips and techniques.

When you become Quietly Powerful, you can contribute your best and make a greater impact on what you care about and you will inspire others to do the same. You will also help the not-so-quiet people to realise that a quieter approach to leadership can be more powerful, particularly as we navigate through complex and ambiguous environments. As more Quietly Powerful leaders emerge, we will bring a more balanced approach to leadership, which I believe is critical for solving some of the biggest challenges we face today.

Part V

For the not-so-quiet people and organisations

IN THIS FINAL part of the book, I would like to encourage the not-so-quiet people to consider the benefits of valuing their quiet nature as a leadership strength for their organisations as well as for themselves.

My encouragement is not intended to value quiet over the not-so-quiet. I have many extroverted, gregarious, outgoing and noisy friends and colleagues, and I love and appreciate them for the energy they bring. Many of them make fantastic leaders as well. It's not about only having Quietly Powerful leaders.

I see it as a balance between the outspoken, confident-looking and dominant style of leadership with the quieter, humble and reflective style. Organisations will benefit from having both and having the different styles complement and work together.

Chapter 18

'So what?' for organisations

The key concern for organisations is whether they have hidden talent going to waste. In an environment where there is a 'war for talent', some fields are suffering from a talent shortage and it seems crazy to be ignoring this hidden talent pool.

It's also irrational to overlook potential Quietly Powerful leaders in organisations, given the positive impact their leadership could have on people in their teams. The leadership gaps described in Chapter 2 do exist in organisations, and maintaining the status quo on leadership will do nothing to address them. While Quietly Powerful leadership is not the 'silver bullet', it will at least change the leadership team dynamics, how teams and organisations are led, and the messages people receive about what kind of leadership is valued in the organisation.

The balancing of leadership styles is particularly important as organisations are faced with a changing and uncertain external environment as well as shifts in the demographic mix within the organisation.

Giovanni Stagno, as mentioned in Chapter 13, explained the need to adapt our leadership style to the changing cultural demographic mix:

> *We've done a number of studies internally about the differences between people of Asian descent with regards to the interdependence that they have with community and family versus what we have in western culture which centres mainly on independence, freedom of speech, and your personal identity… This confirms a leadership style that's not necessarily responsive to the shift of our workforce and, in some cases, that doesn't appeal to those looking for a place to start and grow their career – they're wanting a place that is really, truly global. We need to give people who aren't demonstrating their knowledge by being loud, boisterous or vocal a chance to shine. To somehow elevate their status and give them the freedom to show that they still are very valuable, they have a lot of insight to offer, even though they don't act with what we would typically expect in terms of taking leadership. I try to take people like that, those that didn't naturally fit the mould, and give them a chance.*

Studies show Generation Z workers are invested in positive work environments, with Ryan Jenkins reporting in his article, 'Statistics Exposing What Generation Z Wants from the Workplace', that 77 per cent say a company's diversity would be a deciding factor. Younger generations typically do not respond well to autocratic leadership styles based on positional rank, especially ones where they don't feel included or feel like they are taken seriously. Given that the demographics in organisations are guaranteed to include more of the younger generations, an update in leadership styles is a necessity if we want younger talent to contribute their best.

Here are some ideas on what organisations can do to tap into their quiet talent.

Find and nurture your hidden talent

Some of your hidden talent are likely to be right under your nose. They may not show 'leader-like' behaviours in a traditional sense, but they are often the ones who achieve results, are trusted by many as a 'safe pair of hands' and care about the collective purpose and outcomes. Organisations and leaders need to look for and nurture these talented professionals in a different way.

Find the reluctant leaders, quiet achievers and behind the scenes supporters

During the Quietly Powerful leader interviews I discovered many of them were reluctant leaders. Some did not see themselves as a potential leader and others only stepped into leadership because they were pulled by a cause or meaningful purpose. Many of them had a manager, mentor or a coach who saw their potential. They prompted these potential leaders to consider a leadership position or gave them roles they didn't feel ready for because they believed in them.

Ruth Picker shared her experience as a young professional of being told that she could be a CEO in the future:

> *I never saw myself as being a leader. I was very technical; accounting standards were my thing and that's what I was known for and I wrote a book. One of my wonderful mentors was the CEO of the Australian firm at the time. He said to me, 'You know you could be the CEO of this firm if you wanted to.' I looked at him like he was crazy and I said, 'What? But that's not my core skill.' He said, 'What do you think your core skill is?' I replied, 'Technical stuff, accounting standards.' And he said, 'No, that's not your core skill.' I said, 'Oh? What is it?' He said, 'Your core skill is people; dealing with people is the thing you're best at.' He saw that in me [when] I didn't see that in me.*

Susan Middleditch fell into her first CFO role at the age of 25 when her boss left and told her that she should do his job:

> *When my boss approached me and I walked away from that discussion, I went back to him and gave him a whole list of people that could do the job better than I could. But, as I said, he wasn't taking any of those excuses. He just said to me, 'Look, it's your time. It's a chance for you to step up into that role. You know the team, you know the customers, so you need to give it a go.'*

Susan Allen had similar experiences of not seeing herself as a leader, but having managers who saw her capabilities and encouraged her to take the risk of new roles and situations. She said:

> *[One of my mentors] was a man I worked with for 16 years. He had the capability to make me do things I didn't think I was capable of. He would throw me into situations that were way outside my comfort zone. He once put me in charge of a project to get all of the state automobile clubs to agree to a set of standards for a telematics hub that meant that they could all communicate electronically for road service. So, I was chairing a committee made up entirely of men, on a subject I knew very little about, but he just had absolute confidence that I would get there. And because he did, I was determined to get there and did time and time again.*

Ruth is now a respected Partner at Ernst & Young in the risk management field. Susan Middleditch has had multiple senior executive roles in corporate and government, now holding a Deputy Secretary role at Victoria Police. Susan Allen is a former Executive General Manager reporting to the CEO at RACV. All three have made and continue to make significant contributions to their organisations, clients, customers and stakeholders. If their managers and mentors had not seen their potential, all their talents could have remained hidden.

Additionally, finding and developing potential Quietly Powerful leaders benefits organisations because they become inclusive and attract highly talented people who may be neglected elsewhere.

Helen Macfarlane believes that her organisation, Addisons, attracts and retains some of the best lawyers because they value and recognise their quiet achievers. She spoke of their recent round of promotions:

> *I think the partners were very excited about the promotions including one member of my team who's a quiet achiever and I was the one who actually approached her about putting herself forward for promotion… I was aware that she would be a bit reticent about doing so and she certainly deserved the promotion. She worked very, very hard on developing her skills and her experience, and I was very thrilled when she was successful in the promotion. Some of our lawyers are quiet and may be less attractive to the larger firms who want the big personalities and that's a fantastic windfall for us because they are extraordinary lawyers.*

As an organisational leader, how aware are you of your hidden talent? Do you or your organisation look for the obvious or are you open to different people with different styles?

Work with what works for them

My extrovert friend, Donna, told me about a quiet team member who rarely said anything in meetings and would often share ideas with her after the meeting. Donna became increasingly frustrated that this team member wouldn't share his ideas in the group. After seeing this pattern of behaviour several times, she asked the team member, 'Why didn't you share that in the room when everyone was there? It would have been very useful as part of the discussion. Now we have to go back to the group and discuss it again.'

The team member responded that he was unable to contribute in the team meetings because most of his colleagues were loud and outspoken and he couldn't get a word in. He said that he tried to open his mouth or even raise his hand, but he was ignored or spoken over and the conversation moved on too quickly. Donna pushed back saying that there was space for him to contribute and that he would need to learn to join the conversation at the pace it was going. He responded that he needed help to join the conversation as he had tried a few different approaches and they hadn't worked. He suggested that relevant materials and agenda be sent before the meeting and that the meeting chair deliberately created moments of pause to invite the quieter voices into the discussion. He also suggested that Donna, as the head of the team, observe who might be struggling to enter the discussion.

His response was surprising to Donna, as she was someone who had no trouble inserting herself into conversations. She was able to extract valuable contributions from her team member by making small adjustments to how she ran her meetings.

Quiet professionals find that some of the office environments, systems and processes don't work for them. Some of them even find situations like large group offsites and leadership assessment centres traumatic, as described in Chapter 10. Organisations would benefit from rethinking and redesigning some of these systems and processes to enable quiet professionals to bring out their best. Asking some of your quiet talent about what would work for them would be a great start.

This rethink requires some challenging of our default thinking and assumptions. For example, there is an assumption that collaboration requires people to be together or be able to bump into each other frequently. This was the premise of the open-plan office environment. Given that research is starting to show the contrary, it's time to consider what really drives collaboration. Another assumption is the view that bringing a group together and brainstorming is the best way to generate ideas, but, again, research is rejecting this long-held assumption. Lastly, there are many people screaming against the number of meetings they have to go to, and this isn't just quiet professionals!

'So what?' for organisations

Dr Jason Fox described a gap he sees in most organisations as 'asynchronous communication':

> ...what I see, which is such a big gap in most organisations, is the lack of asynchronous comms. With most organisations, the communication happens via phone calls, meetings and emails. Phone calls are terrible if you're the one receiving the call; it's an interruption. It's fine if you're making the call but there's no legacy of the conversation, no one else knows what you talked about. Meetings – no one wants to have more meetings... but people have so many in their days. And then emails – people have so many emails; their inbox becomes a task management thing. There's no space for complex thinking. But collaboration software and things like Basecamp, Atlassian software and Yammer allow a space for more thoughtfulness and more consideration. I think the more that we can champion that, the more that we're going to have a space for consideration, thoughtfulness and deeper thoughts to emerge where they're very unlikely to emerge in a meeting of an hour's time.

For organisations, do you know if your quiet talent is unable to contribute their best in the current environment? In fact, some of the office set-up may be detrimental to productivity for everyone, not just quiet professionals. Are you open to challenging your assumptions about what environments, systems and processes enhance productivity, creativity and collaboration?

Encourage quiet professionals to be brave

When I posted an article called 'Don't tell me to be more confident' in 2016, I didn't expect people from around the world would respond the way they did. I received comments such as:

> If I had a dollar for each time I've had the 'You need to be more confident' comment... and, yes, it destroys any confidence you did have.

Your article really resonated with me. Every time I've been told 'to be more confident' it just left me feeling confused and unseen.

It made me smile because it reminded me of a recent conversation I had with a male leader. Just as you highlight in your post, I asked him to reflect on what would be the likely outcome of telling his female manager that he wanted her to be more confident – it was a light-bulb moment for him. I also asked him why he wanted her to be more confident. On reflection, he realised that she was doing a great job and role stereotypes were driving his concerns rather than an objective assessment of her ability.

There are problems with telling people to be more confident as discussed in Chapter 8.

Real confidence only grows through action. Courage is what gets people into action when they aren't feeling confident. 'Feel the fear and do it anyway,' as Susan Jeffers wrote in her book of the same name. The best thing that managers, mentors and coaches can do to support the building of confidence is to encourage quiet professionals to be brave and try something new or take on a challenge. If they can find something that aligns with their passions and values, even better. Supporting them to take an experimental approach also helps; starting small, learning from what's worked and what hasn't and then scaling up. The more they learn and make progress, the more they feel confident and comfortable with having a go, which creates a virtuous cycle.

Improve the quality of leadership

Finding, developing and recognising Quietly Powerful leaders will elevate the standards of leadership as advocated by Dr Tomas Chamorro-Premuzic in *Why do so Many Incompetent Men become Leaders?* There are highly competent men and women who are overlooked because they are quieter and humble.

'So what?' for organisations

As explained in Part 1, organisations risk wasting a lot of talent, enduring poor quality leadership and continuing to damage people's wellbeing by undervaluing quiet approaches. In the world of talent shortages, ever-changing and increasingly complex organisational environments and customer expectations, improving the quality of leadership is a high-impact activity to enable organisations to thrive. It's time to challenge our default thinking and beliefs about what to look for in our leaders.

If diversity and inclusion is a high priority for your organisation, or you see some backlash or resistance to making progress, improving the quality of leadership is far more likely to get agreement and support. And who wouldn't want better quality leadership in their organisations?

The challenge now is to redefine what high quality leadership looks, sounds and feels like, while also retraining our minds to get past what we may have been used to. Some practical ideas may include:

- Catch yourself when you're hooked by the awestruck effect described in Chapter 8, resist the initial gut feeling about charismatic and confident-looking people as being more leader-like.

- If you are interviewing a confident-appearing person, deliberately ask more probing questions to understand their competence.

- Watch out for making decisions based on first impressions – especially if they aren't so positive. Counter your confirmation biases by looking for other evidence to the contrary.

- Pay attention to and recognise substance; what people say, do and deliver, not just their style and how they come across.

- Change the selection criteria and system to ensure that you assess actual leadership performance and potential, rather than the effectiveness of their self-promotion and perceived charisma. For example, prioritise feedback and data about their actual leadership effectiveness from people with less power – such as their team members.

- Deliberately look for and recognise the less visible skills and qualities such as the quiet superpowers described in Chapter 14.
- Actively look for potential Quietly Powerful leaders and encourage them to use their quiet strengths and grow.

This change in approach to diversity and inclusion, as well as talent and leadership, will help to reduce the appalling effects of poor leadership in organisations – from the power abuse by leaders, self-interest, greed-based decisions and 'psychopathic' behaviours, to poor engagement, performance and stagnated innovation in organisations.

Chapter 19

'So what?' for not-so-quiet individuals

As I mentioned at the start of Part V, I love and appreciate my not-so-quiet friends and colleagues and I don't want them to change. For the not-so-quiet readers, I wish the same for you and offer my thoughts on how you might work with your quieter colleagues and how you can learn from them.

Balancing of opposites

I have a lot to learn from my noisier friends and colleagues. When we have the opportunity to work together, we complement each other and learn from each other. This isn't just based on how I feel, it's based on feedback from others. When co-facilitating with my extrovert colleagues, I've received feedback from participants about how much they learned from our different styles. Different people have different learning styles and ideas make sense when shared in different ways. By having the contrasting styles, together we cover the broad range of learning styles and ways of sharing concepts.

In my experience, the leadership teams with similar styles and personalities either had a lot of clashes or were too 'nice'. In one leadership team, half the members had a very high will or dominance score. With so many team members wanting their way, their discussions would often end up as arguments that led nowhere. Another leadership team agreed with everything and didn't challenge anything that their peers brought to the table. They were too comfortable and groupthink had become the norm.

Leadership teams with a diversity of styles *did* have the challenges of misunderstanding each other. However, once they appreciated their differences and how to get the best out of each other, they actively looked for ways to work together. Collaboration became meaningful, as they knew it would be valuable for everyone involved. The teams that learned to handle disagreements and how to listen to contrary views also benefited from being able to test their thinking and assumptions.

The benefits are there to be extracted by everyone making some adaptations to accommodate different styles. For those who are vocal, having some patience and asking what works for the quieter team members will pay dividends for you and for them. It's also helpful to acknowledge and amend any systemic biases against quieter team members.

Sharing what you need from the quieter team members is useful. For example, your quiet colleague may be completely unaware that you get worried that they appear disinterested when they go quiet. It takes two to tango, as they say, so it's important to request any adjustments, as well as offering to make adjustments yourself.

There is so much to be gained through mutual understanding and adjusting. I believe this is the path to true inclusion. Rather than making assumptions about what women need, what the younger generation expects or how to help LGBTQI+ members to feel included, have conversations to understand the needs at an individual level. Each individual has a complex mix of identities, personalities and conditioning. True inclusion is about making the most of these differences.

Find quiet within yourself

Something I've noticed is that many of my not-so-quiet friends and colleagues whom I admire have developed their ability to access their quiet side. Many of them meditate, are good listeners and have worked on themselves enough to have that inner confidence. Some of them have told me that they value their quiet time more than they used to as they've gotten older.

For example, when I have conversations with friends who are very aware of their chattier tendencies, I find that they would usually speak first for a while, but then take the time to stop and really listen to me when I talked, as well as asking a few questions. Because of their awareness when they're speaking, I feel comfortable to ask questions or jump in if I have something useful to share.

Usually they'll speak for 60 to 80 per cent of the time, but I'm happy with that. I get to find out more about them and learn from them. I don't feel the need to share everything and anything.

What I know is that these friends have found their own version of quiet within themselves. They value and actively seek out quiet time, whether it's through meditation, yoga, retreats, nature walks, art or some kind of time-out activities. Some of them spend time on reflection and journalling. They know that quiet is essential to their well-being.

So, if you're a not-so-quiet person and find that you haven't been prioritising quiet space in your life, I encourage you to learn from your quiet friends and colleagues. Find out what they do to re-energise and create space. Perhaps have a night in rather than a night out sometimes. Find time and space for solitude.

You don't have to be naturally quiet to access the quiet superpowers. *You* can also go on the journey of Quietly Powerful by becoming more comfortable with yourself, learning to be present and committing to a purpose or mission that determines your behaviours. You can then consciously access your quiet nature and apply it to your daily routines and activities. I think you'll like it and you might find that others like your quieter side, too.

Helping future generations

A mother of two teenage children spoke up at one of my public breakfasts after hearing the challenges of being a quieter professional. She said that her son was the popular, outgoing type who had lots of friends, while her daughter was the quieter type. She spoke of a time when her daughter came to her teary-eyed and said, 'What's wrong with me, Mum? Why aren't I like my brother?' She said that it was difficult to answer her question, as she herself felt disadvantaged by her quiet nature.

If we set an example as parents, family members, friends and colleagues of valuing our own quiet natures, then children like this quiet girl won't feel like there's anything wrong with being quiet. We need to teach them that finding quiet and stillness within is just as important a skill as relating and socialising, and it should be just as valuable as our sociable nature. Human beings are social *and* solitary creatures.

In fact, having access to a quiet mind improves our ability to relate to each other, as we can be more present. By doing this, we can help our future generations feel pride in their quiet nature while also feeling more balanced.

My wish, in conclusion

Ultimately, Quietly Powerful is a state that can be accessed by anyone – whether you are naturally quiet or not.

Given the rates of burnout and anxiety in this noisy, busy world, my wish is that more people find the quiet, still, peaceful power within themselves. Given the frequency of miscommunication and frustrations that follow, my wish is that more people find the quiet space to listen deeply. Given the sense of hopelessness or helplessness with the vast range of problems we see in the world, my wish is that more people connect with something bigger than themselves to give them a sense of purpose, quiet optimism and peace. Given the leadership gaps we are seeing today, my wish is that more Quietly Powerful leaders emerge and lift the overall quality of leadership in the world.

Quietly Powerful is a state of being at peace with yourself. So, as I always say at the end of my Quietly Powerful presentation, my wish for you is to…

Play the music you were born to play.

About the author

Megumi is an author, speaker and consultant in leadership, culture, diversity and inclusion, with a background in strategy, economics and finance. With a client list that includes Addisons, Computershare, Department of Health and Human Services, Ernst & Young, JBWere, National Australia Bank, Roche, Sanofi, SEEK, and smaller for-profit, government and not-for-profit organisations, Megumi expands leaders' mindsets and skillsets to inspire diverse talent to flourish. In her first book, *Start Inspiring, Stop Driving: Unlock your team's potential to outperform and grow*, she shares how leaders can unlock their potential by being smart together, not on their own.

In the uncertain, changing, global and interconnected world, Megumi believes that the 'alpha' or 'hero' leadership style alone is outdated and inadequate. Her Quietly Powerful movement aims to expand the definition of good leadership while empowering quieter professionals and those outside majority groups to fulfil their potential.

Megumi is also a busy dance mum for her passionate ballet-dancer daughter. The art of ballet has influenced her thinking, as she has learned more about how powerful a dancer needs to be to quietly and elegantly hold ballet positions. Some of the slowest, easiest looking movements are actually the most difficult to perform.

For more information about the Quietly Powerful movement, go to:

- Website – www.megumimiki.com
- Megumi's personal LinkedIn – au.linkedin.com/in/megumimiki
- Quietly Powerful LinkedIn – www.linkedin.com/groups/7065506
- Twitter – @megumimiki1

Sources and further reading

Chapter 1

Naidu, Yamini (2016) *Power Play: Game changing influence strategies for leaders*, Wiley, Australia.

Pollard, Matthew (2018) *The Introvert's Edge: How the Quiet and Shy Can Outsell Anyone*, American Management Association, New York.

Chapter 2

Beck, Randall and Harter, Jim (2014) 'Why Good Managers Are So Rare', Harvard Business Review. https://hbr.org/2014/03/why-good-managers-are-so-rare

Chamorro-Premuzic, Dr Tomas (2019) *'Why Do So Many Incompetent Men Become Leaders? (and how to fix it)*, Harvard Business Review Press, Boston.

Commonwealth of Australia (2019) 'Final Report of the Royal Commission into Misconduct in the Banking, Superannuation and Financial Services Industry' https://treasury.gov.au/sites/default/files/2019-03/fsrc-volume1.pdf

Commonwealth of Australia (2017) 'Royal Commission into Institutional Responses to Child Sexual Abuse' https://www.childabuseroyalcommission.gov.au/final-report

Covey, Stephen R. (1989) *The 7 Habits of Highly Effective People*, Free Press, New York.

D'Souza, Steven and Renner, Diana (2014) *Not Knowing: The Art of Effortless Action*, LID Publishing, London.

Fox, Dr Jason (2015) *How to Lead a Quest: A Handbook for Pioneering Executives*, Wiley, Australia.

Grant, Adam (2019) 'Power doesn't corrupt. It just exposes who leaders really are', *Washington Post*, https://www.washingtonpost.com/business/economy/power-doesnt-corrupt-it-just-exposes-who-leaders-really-are/2019/02/22/

f5680116-3600-11e9-854a-7a14d7fec96a_story.html?noredirect=on&utm_term=.917bc057719a.

Grant, Adam, Gino, Francesca and Hoffman, David A. (2010) 'The Hidden Advantages of Quiet Bosses', *Harvard Business Review*. https://hbr.org/2010/12/the-hidden-advantages-of-quiet-bosses

Gregersen, Hal (2017) 'Being Quiet Is Part of Being a Good CEO', *The Atlantic*.

Groysberg, Boris and Bell, Deborah (2013) 'Talent management: Boards give their companies an 'F'', https://hbr.org/2013/05/talent-management-boards-give.

Heifetz, Ron and Linsky, Marty (2009) *The Practice of Adaptive Leadership: Tools and Tactics for Changing Your Organization and the World*, Harvard Business Review Press, Massachusetts.

Kahneman, Daniel (2011) *Thinking Fast and Slow*, Farrar, Straus and Giroux, New York.

Keltner Dr Dacher (2016) *The Power Paradox: How we gain and lose influence*, Penguin Books, London.

Keltner Dr Dacher (2007) 'The Power Paradox', *Greater Good Magazine*. https://greatergood.berkeley.edu/article/item/power_paradox

Kets de Vries, Manfred F.R. (2016) 'Do you hate your boss?' https://hbr.org/product/do-you-hate-your-boss/R1612H-PDF-ENG.

Knowledge@Wharton (2010) 'Analyzing Effective Leaders: Why Extraverts Are Not Always the Most Successful Bosses'. http://knowledge.wharton.upenn.edu/article/analyzing-effective-leaders-why-extraverts-are-not-always-the-most-successful-bosses/

Lam, Bourree (2017) *Being quiet is part of being a good CEO*, The Atlantic., https://www.theatlantic.com/business/archive/2017/03/qa-hal-gregersen/518460/.

Lustig, Dr Robert (2009) University of California Television 'Sugar: The Bitter Truth'. https://www.youtube.com/watch?v=dBnniua6-oM

McGregor, Jena (2017) 'How too much focus on 'superstar' workers enable harassment', *Washington Post*. https://www.washingtonpost.com/pb/news/on-leadership/wp/2017/12/19/the-metoo-movement-is-a-warning-sign-about-the-star-system-

Sources and further reading

at-many-companies/?commentID=&outputType=comment&utm_term=.6742037d4031

Menzies, Felicity (2016) *A World of Difference*, Major Street Publishing, Australia.

Nolan, Tom, 'The No. 1 Employee Benefit That No One's Talking About', Gallup. https://www.gallup.com/workplace/232955/no-employee-benefit-no-one-talking.aspx?g_source=link_wwwv9&g_campaign=item_246080&g_medium=copy.

Riffkin, Rebecca and Harter, Jim (2016) 'Using Employee Engagement to Build a Diverse Workforce', Gallup. https://news.gallup.com/opinion/gallup/190103/using-employee-engagement-build-diverse-workforce.aspx.

Sutton, Robert (2017) *The A--hole Survival Guide: How to deal with people who treat you like dirt*, Penguin Books, London.

Tett, Gillian (2019) 'More chief executives are paying for their ethical mis-steps', *Financial Times*. https://www.ft.com/content/490c12e4-7cab-11e9-81d2-f785092ab560

Wikipedia regarding Ancel Keys. https://en.wikipedia.org/wiki/Ancel_Keys

Yudkin, John (1972) *Pure, White and Deadly: The Problem of Sugar*, Davis-Poynter, London

Chapter 3

Australian Psychological Society and Swinburne University of Technology (2018) 'Australian Loneliness Report'. https://psychweek.org.au/wp/wp-content/uploads/2018/11/Psychology-Week-2018-Australian-Loneliness-Report.pdf

Dobrygowski, Daniel (2016) 'This is the one key trait that all great leaders share', World Economic Forum. https://www.weforum.org/agenda/2016/03/key-trait-all-great-leaders-share/

Gross, Daniel A. (2014) 'This Is Your Brain on Silence', Nautilus. http://nautil.us/issue/16/nothingness/this-is-your-brain-on-silence

Jennings-Edquist, Grace (2018) 'Feeling isolated? You're not alone. Here's why 1 in 4 of us is lonely', ABC Life. https://www.abc.net.au/life/social-isolation-why-are-we-so-lonely/10493414

Kahneman, Daniel (2011) *Thinking Fast and Slow*, Farrar, Straus and Giroux, New York.

Kelland, Kate (2018) 'Mental health crisis could cost the world $16 trillion by 2030', Reuters. https://www.reuters.com/article/us-health-mental-global/mental-health-crisis-could-cost-the-world-16-trillion-by-2030-idUSKCN1MJ2QN

Kethledge, Raymond and Erwin, Michael S. (2017) *Lead Yourself First: Inspiring leadership through solitude*, Bloomsbury, London.

Lawton, Richard (2017) *Raise Your Voice: Transforming how you speak, sing and present*, Finch, Australia.

Mindfulnet.org, Research relating to mindfulness at work (reference to paper by Pykett, Jessica, Lilley, Rachel, Whitehead, Mark, Howell, Rachel and Jones, Rhys (2016) 'Mindfulness, Behaviour Change and Decision Making: An Experimental Trial'). http://www.mindfulnet.org/page18.htm

Schwartz, Roger (2013) *Smart Leaders, Smarter Teams: How You and Your Team Get Unstuck to Get Results*, Jossey-Bass, San Francisco.

Scott, Susan (2002) *Fierce Conversations: Achieving Success at Work and in Life One Conversation at a Time*, Berkeley, New York.

Talbot-Zorn, Justin and Marz, Leigh (2017) 'The busier you are, the more you need quiet time', *Harvard Business Review*. https://hbr.org/2017/03/the-busier-you-are-the-more-you-need-quiet-time

Trimboli, Oscar (2017) *Deep Listening: How to make an impact beyond words*, Oscar Trimboli, Australia.

VicHealth (2015) *Survey: Young Victorians' resilience & mental wellbeing*. https://www.vichealth.vic.gov.au/young-victorians-survey

Wigert, Ben and Agrawal, Sangeeta (2018) 'Employee Burnout, Part 1: The 5 Main Causes', Gallup. https://www.gallup.com/workplace/237059/employee-burnout-part-main-causes.aspx.

World Health Organisation (2019) 'International Classification of Diseases and Related Health Problems'. https://icd.who.int/browse11/l-m/en#/http://id.who.int/icd/entity/129180281

Yoshino, Kenji (2014) 'Diversity Does Not Mean Having to Choose Between Identity and Inclusion', Big Think. https://bigthink.com/think-tank/kenji-yoshino-diversity.

Sources and further reading

Chapter 4

Ancowitz, Nancy (2012) 'APA Gains Sanity: Introverts Not Nuts', *Psychology Today*. https://www.psychologytoday.com/au/blog/self-promotion-introverts/201206/apa-gains-sanity-introverts-not-nuts

Aron, Elaine (1999) *The Highly Sensitive Person: How to thrive when the world overwhelms you*, Thorsons, New York.

Cain, Susan (2012) *Quiet: The power of introverts in a world that can't stop talking*, Crown Publishing Group, New York.

Helgoe, Laurie (2013) *Introvert Power: Why your inner life is your hidden strength*, Sourcebooks, Illinois.

Kahnweiler, Jennifer (2013) *The Introvert Leader: Building on your quiet strength*, Berrett-Koehler Publishers, San Francisco.

Kuofie, Matthew, Stephens-Craig, Dana and Dool, Richard (2015) 'An Overview Perception of Introverted Leaders', *International Journal of Global Business*. https://docplayer.net/21812339-An-overview-perception-of-introverted-leaders.html

Little, Dr Brian (2016) *Me, Myself and Us: The science of personality and the art of well-being*, Public Affairs, New York.

Pollard, Matthew (2018) *The Introvert's Edge: How the quiet and shy can outsell anyone*, American Management Association, New York.

Chapter 5

BBC documentary (2018) 'No More Boys And Girls: Can our kids go gender free?' https://www.youtube.com/watch?v=wN5R2LWhTrY&t=1941s

Chamorro-Premuzic, Dr Tomas (2018) *Why Do So Many Incompetent Men Become Leaders? (and how to fix it)*, Harvard Business Review Press, Boston.

Fox, Catherine (2017) *Stop Fixing Women: Why building fairer workplaces is everybody's business*, University of New South Wales Press, Australia.

Hofstede, Prof. Geert, Hofstede Insights website with information about cultural differences between countries. https://www.hofstede-insights.com/

Pappert, Tom (2019) 'Woman Who Media Claims Created Black Hole Image Contributed 0.26% of Code'. https://bigleaguepolitics.com/woman-who-media-claims-created-black-hole-image-contributed-0-26-of-code/

Chapter 6

Cantieri, Becky (2018) *How to measure Diversity and Inclusion for a stronger workplace*, Surveymonkey. https://www.surveymonkey.com/mp/diversity-and-inclusion-guide/

Diamond, Dr Julie (2016) *Power: A user's guide*, Belly Song Press, New Mexico.

Safe Work Australia (2017) 'National Data Set for Bullying and Harassment in Australian Workplaces'. https://www.safeworkaustralia.gov.au/doc/infographic-workplace-bullying-and-violence

Wikipedia article for the #MeToo movement. https://en.m.wikipedia.org/wiki/Me_Too_movement

Chapter 7

Holmes, Oliver Wendell Holmes Snr (1865) From the poem 'The Voiceless' in *Autocrat of the Breakfast Table*

Chapter 8

Brown, Brené (2010) 'The Power of Vulnerability', TED Talk. https://www.ted.com/talks/Brené_brown_on_vulnerability?language=en

Chamorro-Premuzic, Dr Tomas (2019) *Why Do So Many Incompetent Men Become Leaders? (and how to fix it)*, Harvard Business Review Press, Boston.

Cliffe, Sarah (2015) 'Leadership Qualities' vs Competence: Which Matters More?', *Harvard Business Review* (on research by Lindred Greer from Stanford University, Murat Tarakci and Patrick Groenen from the Rotterdam School of Management)

Collins, Jim (2001) *Good to Great, Why some companies make the leap... and others don't*, William Collins, New York.

Sources and further reading

Dean, Jeremy (2016) 'Being A Narcissist And Having High Self-Esteem Are Totally Different Things', PsyBlog. https://www.spring.org.uk/2016/03/narcissism-self-esteem-difference.php

Dunning, David and Kruger, Justin (2009) 'Unskilled and Unaware of It: How difficulties in recognizing one's own incompetence lead to inflated self-assessments', Psychology. https://www.researchgate.net/publication/12688660_Unskilled_and_Unaware_of_It_How_Difficulties_in_Recognizing_One's_Own_Incompetence_Lead_to_Inflated_Self-Assessments

Grant, Adam (2013) *Give and Take: Why helping others drives our success*, Penguin Books, New York.

Grant, Adam, Gino, Francesca and Hofmann, Gino (2011) 'Reversing the Extraverted Leadership Advantage: The Role of Employee Proactivity', *Academy of Management Journal*.

Greenleaf, Robert K. (1977) S*ervant Leadership: A journey into the nature of legitimate power and greatness*, Paulist Press, New York.

Hunt, Vivian, Yee, Lareina, Prince, Sara, and Dixon-Fyle, Sundiatu (2018) 'Delivering through diversity', McKinsey & Company. https://www.mckinsey.com/business-functions/organization/our-insights/delivering-through-diversity?cid=other-eml-nsl-mip-mck-oth-1802

Kahneman, Daniel (2011) *Thinking Fast and Slow*, Farrar, Straus and Giroux, New York.

McSweeney, Linda (2018) 'It's official: Power creates a narcissist', The University of Melbourne Pursuit. https://pursuit.unimelb.edu.au/articles/it-s-official-power-creates-a-narcissist

Menges, Jochen et al (2015) 'The Awestruck Effect: Followers suppress emotion expression in response to charismatic but not individually considerate leadership', *The Leadership Quarterly*.

Nasher, Jack (2019) 'To seem more competent, be more confident', *Harvard Business Review*. https://hbr.org/2019/03/to-seem-more-competent-be-more-confident

Shellenbarger, Sue (2018) 'The best bosses are humble bosses', *Wall Street Journal*. https://www.wsj.com/articles/the-best-bosses-are-humble-bosses-1539092123

Taylor, Bill (2018) 'If humility is so important, why are leaders so arrogant?', *Harvard Business Review*. https://hbr.org/2018/10/if-humility-is-so-important-why-are-leaders-so-arrogant

Chapter 9

Block, Peter (2013) *Stewardship: Choosing Service over Self-Interest*, Berrett-Koehler Publishers, California.

Scouller, James (2016) *The Three Levels of Leadership: How to develop your leadership presence, Knowhow and Skill*, Management Books 2000, United Kingdom.

Scouller, James (2016) 'Why we don't get the political leaders we need?' http://www.three-levels-of-leadership.com/blog/self-mastery-2/why-dont-we-get-the-political-leaders-we-need/2016/12/19/#more-3780

Chapter 10

Furnham, Adrian (2000) 'The Brainstorming Myth', Semantic Scholar. https://pdfs.semanticscholar.org/a2f4/5b4a13c822f1710338670693bcd233aef987.pdf

Padley, Ann (2016) 'For more effective brainstorming, use a hybrid approach'. https://www.annpadley.com/musings/2016/4/26/effective-brainstorming-using-a-hybrid-approach.

Talbot-Zorn, Justin and Marz, Leigh (2017) 'The busier you are, the more you need quiet time'. https://hbr.org/2017/03/the-busier-you-are-the-more-you-need-quiet-time

The Conversation (2018) 'Open offices make people talk less and email more', BBC capital. http://www.bbc.com/capital/story/20180718-open-offices-make-people-talk-less-and-email-more

Chapter 11

Chamorro-Premuzic, Dr Tomas (2019) *Why Do So Many Incompetent Men Become Leaders? (and how to fix it)*, Harvard Business Review Press, Boston.

Hill, Jenny (2017) 'Angela Merkel's quiet power', BBC. https://www.bbc.co.uk/news/resources/idt-sh/angela_merkel

Kimmel, Michael (2015) 'Why gender equality is good for everyone',

Sources and further reading

TED Talk. https://www.ted.com/talks/michael_kimmel_why_gender_equality_is_good_for_everyone_men_included?language=en

Parks, Jason (2011) 'Study Finds Cars Designed to Protect Men, Not Women', Auto Know. https://blog.safeauto.com/study-finds-cars-designed-to-protect-men-not-women/

Plum Village website, biography of Thich Nhat Hanh. https://plumvillage.org/about/thich-nhat-hanh/biography/

Renner, Diana and D'Souza, Steven (2018) *Not Doing: The art of effortless action*, LID Publishing, London.

Chapter 16

Brown, Brené (2018) *Dare to Lead: Brave work. Tough conversations. Whole hearts*, Ebury Publishing, London.

Brown, Brené (2015) *Daring Greatly: How the courage to be vulnerable transforms the way we live, love, parent, and lead*, Avery, New York.

Brown, Brené (2010) *Gifts of Imperfection: Let go of who you think you're supposed to be and embrace who you are*, Hazelden Publishing, Minnesota.

Childre, Doc Lew and Martin, Howard (2000) *The HeartMath Solution: The Institute of HeartMath's Revolutionary Program for Engaging the Power of the Heart's Intelligence*, HarperCollins Publishers Inc, New York.

Dweck, Dr Carol (2006) *Mindset: The new psychology of success*, Ballantine Books, New York.

Little, Dr Brian (2016) *Me, Myself and Us: The science of personality and the art of well-being*, Public Affairs, New York.

South Central Strategic Health Authority and the Welsh Government, Introverted Leadership Toolkit. http://www.introvertedleaders.co.uk/

Riggio, Ronald (2012) 'There's Magic in Your Smile', *Psychology Today*. https://www.psychologytoday.com/au/blog/cutting-edge-leadership/201206/there-s-magic-in-your-smile

Chapter 17

Brown, Brené (2018) *Dare to Lead: Brave work. Tough conversations. Whole hearts*, Ebury Publishing, London.

Brown, Brené (2015) *Daring Greatly: How the courage to be vulnerable transforms the way we live, love, parent, and lead*, Avery, New York.

Brown, Brené (2010) *Gifts of Imperfection: Let go of who you think you're supposed to be and embrace who you are*, Hazelden Publishing, Minnesota.

Childre, Doc Lew and Martin, Howard (2000) *The HeartMath Solution: The Institute of HeartMath's Revolutionary Program for Engaging the Power of the Heart's Intelligence*, HarperCollins Publishers Inc, New York.

Cuddy, Amy (2015) *Presence: Bringing your boldest self to your biggest challenges*, Orion, London.

Elsesser, Kim (2018) 'Power Posing Is Back: Amy Cuddy successfully refutes criticism', *Forbes*. https://www.forbes.com/sites/kimelsesser/2018/04/03/power-posing-is-back-amy-cuddy-successfully-refutes-criticism/#37a1ff873b8e

Chapter 18

Chamorro-Premuzic, Dr Tomas (2019) *Why Do So Many Incompetent Men Become Leaders? (and how to fix it)*, Harvard Business Review Press, Boston.

Jenkins, Ryan, 'Statistics exposing what Generation Z wants from the workplace'. https://blog.ryan-jenkins.com/statistics-exposing-what-generation-z-wants-from-the-workplace

Miki, Megumi (2016) 'Don't tell me to "Be more confident"'. https://www.linkedin.com/pulse/dont-tell-me-more-confident-megumi-miki/

Index

A World of Difference 33
Abdelmoneim, Javid 75
accountability 38, 198
adapting purposefully 164-165, 187-209
adjusting your surroundings 202-204
Adler, Fiona 179, 199, 202
agreeableness 64-65
Allen, Susan 17, 141, 143, 169, 193, 216
alpha leadership 93, 114, 209
anxiety 44-45, 67, 135, 189
appreciating fully 163-164, 169, 171-186, 204
Ardern, Jacinta 111
Aron, Elaine 68
Asahi 73
Asia Professionals Network 7
Asian cultures 69-71, 72, 97-98
assessment centres 118
attention seekers 107
attention-avoidant tendencies 97
Australian Banking Royal Commission 24, 32
authenticity 43-44, 107, 141, 142
autocratic leadership 214
awestruck effect 105-106

Barr, Stacey 139, 192
Bell, Deborah 22
Bellin, Gita xii
biased thinking 117
Big Five personality traits 62, 63, 66
Bird, Jane 16
blind CVs 117
Block, Peter 115, 116
boards 22, 27
Boasman, Paul 18, 61, 141
Bouman, Katie 72-73
brain plasticity 177
brainstorming 121, 122
brave, encouragment to be 219-220
Brockis, Dr Jenny 46, 142, 150, 199
Brown, Brené 110, 170
burnout 44, 45

Cain, Susan 44, 60
CALMER leadership principles 157
career limiting moves 81
centre of attention 188
CEO turnover 26
cerebral palsy 87, 88
challenging authority 70-71

Chamorro-Premuzic, Dr Tomas 23, 76, 102, 127, 220
Chan, Brad 94, 145
charismatic leadership 102, 105-106, 114
childhood experiences 78-79
Clinton, Hillary 108
coaching 66, 155
collaboration 218, 224
collective wisdom 146
comfortable, being 139-140
communication, poor 52-55
competence 103-105
confidence 4, 95, 102-105, 139, 220, 225
confirmation bias 71, 102, 118, 221
contrary opinions, expressing 86-87
courage 110, 170, 189, 220
Covey, Stephen 33
creativity 27, 51, 121
cross-cultural psychology 72
Cuddy, Amy 207, 208, 209
cultural complexity 32-33
cultural diversity 128
cultural fit 108
cultural intelligence 33
culture 4, 40, 69-71

D'Souza, Steven 28, 125
de Silva, Aneetha 146, 201, 203
decision-making 30-32
default thinking 52
Diamond, Julie 80

dietary guidelines 30-31
disabilities, people with 82, 88, 96, 148
diverse talent 117
diversity 40-41, 149, 221
dominance 101-102, 118
dominating leaders 37
Dool, Richard 60
Dunning, David 104
Dweck, Carol 167

ego 24, 26
emotionality 65-67
employee engagement 22
empowering people 38, 155
engaging with people 201
entrepreneurs 26
Erwin, Michael S. 50, 51
ethnic diversity 33, 128
Evans, Lisa 17, 83, 146, 150
expectations of leaders 115
extroverts 7, 60, 61, 69, 106

faking 168
fear 103, 135-136
feedback 52, 81, 119, 103, 104, 134, 140
female leaders 113
Fierce Conversations 54
first impressions 102
Flanagan, Anne ix, 185
focusing 156
Fox, Catherine 76
Fox, Dr Jason 31, 51, 142, 162, 184, 219
Free Trait theory 63, 187
Furnham, Adrian 121

Index

Gallup research 22, 40, 45
gender stereotypes 74-76
Grant, Adam 25, 39, 108
Greenleaf, Robert 109
Greer, Patrick 102
Gregersen, Hal 27
group discussions 156
group dynamics 146
group work 118, 121
groupthink 121
Groysberg, Boris 22

Hanh, Thich Nhat 126
Harrington, Simon 29, 39, 74, 194
Heifetz, Ron 31
Helgoe, Laurie 60
hidden talent 8, 213, 215-220
hiding parts of ourselves 87-88
highly sensitive people 67-68
high-performing teams 145
Hodgkinson, Dr Steve 38, 125, 140, 148, 149
Hofman, David 39
Hofstede, Geert 72, 73
holding yourself back 92-98
Homes, Oliver Wendell 97
How to Lead a Quest 31
humility 29, 104, 109-110, 139, 154

Importance of Women breakfasts 206-207
inclusion 128, 149, 162, 221
inclusivity, perceptions of 40
increasing visibility 197-199
independent thinking 119

Indigenous people 145
influencing 18-19, 155
inner voices 174-176, 177, 179, 181
inside-out development 160, 162, 205-206
internalised marginalisation 95-96, 161, 180
introjections 95
introversion 39, 59-63, 97, 162, 198
Introvert Leader, The 60
Introvert Power 60
Introvert's Edge, The 19, 60

Jacobs, Dianne 139, 193, 197
Japan 2, 69
Japanese attributes 13, 134, 182
Jenkins, Ryan 214
Jung, Carl 61

Kahneman, Daniel 32, 49, 108
Kahnweiler, Jennifer 60
Keltner, Dr Dacher 25
Kethledge, Raymond 50, 51
Kets de Vries, Manfred F.R. 22
Keys, Ancel 30
Kimmel, Michael 127
Kirste, Imke 50
Kruger, Justin 104
Kuofie, Matthew 60

Lancet, The 46
Larkins, Kevin 144
Lawton, Richard 54
Lead Yourself First 50, 51
leadership
– contrasting styles 224

- frameworks 118
- gap 22-42, 213
- mismatches 101
- outdated beliefs 113-116
- quality 15, 220-222
- roles 23

LGBTIQ+ community 83, 96, 224
Linsky, Marty 31
listening 28-30, 33, 109, 125, 143, 144, 153, 154
- poor 34-35, 53
Little, Dr Brian 63
loneliness 48-49
Lowy, Mark 34
Lustig, Dr Robert 30

Macfarlane, Helen 35, 36, 41, 200, 217
managing perceptions 193-194
managing your nerves 207
McClure, Tim 34
McGovern, George 30
Mead, Nicole 106
meditation 45, 47, 205, 207, 225
meetings 120-122, 218
mental health 44-45, 47
Menzies, Felicity 33
Merkel, Angela 126
#metoo movement 90
Michelle, Grocock 93, 186, 188, 189, 191, 196
Middleditch, Susan 85, 185, 188, 191, 193, 216
mindfulness 47, 125, 126, 205
mindset 167-168
minority outsiders 84-85

miscommunications 33
multi-national organisations 33
music 97

Naidu, Yamini 13, 19, 61, 141, 142, 161
narcissism 33, 106
Nasher, Jack 103
natural qualities 114, 173-174
Network of Winning Women 7
networking 142, 189, 200-201
neuroscientists 75, 177
noisy work environments 14, 46, 47, 120
Not Doing 125
Not Knowing 28
not-so-quiet individuals 8, 128, 223-226

office environments 119-120, 127
one-on-one relationships 145, 146
outside in, working from the 206-208
overconfidence 102
overlooking quiet professionals 162
over-simplifying 30-31

parent–child relationship 115
Parks, Rosa 18-19
Paskevicius, Angie 147,
patriarchal leadership 115
perception gap 193
perception of quiet leaders 124-125
personal brand 21

Index

personality 59-68
- assessment tools 62
- profiling 117

Peter, Clive 32, 35, 36, 38, 140, 147, 198, 200
Petriglieri, Gianpiero 50
Picker, Ruth 143, 146, 157, 189, 190, 191, 194, 215, 216
Pollard, Matthew 19, 60
positional leaders 37
Power Distance Index (PDI) 73-74
power dynamics 80-91
Power Paradox, The 25
Power Play 14, 19
power posing 207-208
Practice of Adaptive Leadership, The 31
presence 204-205
present, being 143, 146, 147, 153
presenting 4, 66, 207
problem-solving 14, 89, 156
professional woman survey 14
promotion 96, 117-118
Proust, Elizabeth 27, 28, 198
public speaking 17, 106, 146, 150, 188
Pure, White and Deadly 30
purposeful, being 147-148
Pykett, Jessica 47

questioning 154
quiet achievers 36, 37
quiet leaders, three attributes of 151-152
quiet nature 6, 8, 14

quiet professional women 6-7
quiet reflection 53
quiet space 52, 126
quiet workplaces 127
quiet, finding your 225
quiet, is it a disadvantage? 14
quietly powerful attributes 138-152
quietness
- as a weakness 15-16
- misunderstanding of 16-20

recovery time 203
recruitment 118
reflection 28, 143, 153
reframing strengths and weaknesses 177-179
relationship building 154
religious upbringing 77-78
reluctant leaders 215
Renner, Diana 28, 125
Royal Commission into Institutional Responses to Child Sexual Abuse 24-25

Schuitevoerder, Stephen Dr 82-83
Schwartz, Roger 53
Scott, Susan 54
Scouller, James 114, 116
self-assessment 159-160
self-awareness 133-135
self-doubt 67
self-esteem 104
self-interest 24-26
self-promotion 20-21, 37, 50-51, 107, 124, 180

selling 19, 156
Seven Countries Study 30
Shellenbarger, Sue 111
shrinking 166
silence 50, 54, 126, 154, 155
soft power 13
solitude 50, 68, 225
Speaking Savvy 17
speaking up 194-196
Stagno, Giovanni 40, 144, 214
Stainkamph, Caroline 134, 145, 197, 206
Stephens-Craig, Dana 60
stereotypes 60, 71-72, 119
stewardship 115
Stop Fixing Women 76
storytelling 172-173
Strategy& 26
stress 67
sugar 30-31
summarising 196-197
superpowers 153-157
Sutton, Robert 25
Sydney Japanese International School 2
System 1 thinking 51-52, 108
systemic biases 127

talent management 15, 22, 39-42
tall poppy syndrome 71

Taoists 206
Taylor, Bill 110
teamwork 29
Thinking, Fast and Slow 32, 49, 108
thriving 169-170
Thunberg, Greta 18-19
Timboli, Oscar 53, 124, 195
transparency 144
trust 34-35, 154-155

unconscious bias 37, 75, 101, 118, 119
understanding yourself 172-173
uniqueness, leveraging your 183-186
upbringing 69-79

values 220
valuing your real self 161
Vic ICT 7, 134, 206
vulnerability 103, 104, 110-111, 141, 142

Webb, Katrina 87, 203, 206
workplace bullying 83-84
World Health Organization 45, 46, 60

yoga 45, 206, 225
Yudkin, John 30